THE GREAT WALL

THE GREAT WALL

A Cultural History

CARLOS ROJAS

Harvard University Press

Cambridge, Massachusetts

London, England

2010

Library of Congress Cataloging-in-Publication Data

Rojas, Carlos, 1970–
The Great Wall : a cultural history / Carlos Rojas.
p.   cm.
Includes bibliographical references and index.
ISBN-13: 978-0-674-04787-7 (alk. paper)
ISBN-10: 0-674-04787-7 (alk. paper)
1. Great Wall of China (China)—History.
2. China—Civilization.
I. Title.
DS793.G67R65 2010
951—dc22   2010024946

For Eileen

Contents

Illustrations

Selected Chronology

Pre-imperial period
Shang dynasty ca. 1600–1046 BCE
Zhou dynasty 1045–256

Warring States period
475–221 BCE

Imperial period
Qin dynasty 221–206 BCE
Han dynasty 206 BCE–220 CE

Southern and Northern
dynasties 420–589

Sui dynasty 581–618
Tang dynasty 618–907
Song dynasty 960–1279

Liao dynasty 907–1125

  Northern Song 960–1127
  Southern Song 1127–1279
Yuan dynasty 1271–1368
Ming dynasty 1368–1644
Qing dynasty 1644–1911

Jin dynasty 1115–1234

Modern period
Republic of China 1912–1949
People's Republic of China
  1949–present

Republic of China (Taiwan)
  1949–present

On Names

If names be not rectified, language will not be in accordance with
the truth of things.

—Confucius, *The Analects*

Names are prickly creatures, which Confucius contended must be
firmly "rectified" for language to maintain its proper function and
truth. The problem, however, is that a word, as Justice Oliver
Wendell Holmes once observed, "is not a crystal, transparent and
unchanged; it is the skin of a living thought and may vary greatly in
color and content according to the circumstances and time in which
it is used." In a similar spirit, I have endeavored to make this volume as accurate and accessible as possible while preserving the "living thought" of the language I employ.

In general I use standard English translations of Chinese words,
phrases, and titles of works. With the exception of a handful of
names—like Sun Yat-sen and Chiang Kai-shek—that are better
known under alternate spellings, I use the pinyin transliteration system throughout, and have silently revised quotations from other
modern texts to conform to this system (while preserving, for historical purposes, the original spellings in passages taken from pre-
twentieth-century texts).

I follow the Chinese convention of listing family names before given names, with the exception of a few expatriate authors who have adopted Westernized versions of their names (such as Hualing Nieh, whose surname is Nieh). Chinese emperors traditionally have at least three names: a personal name, the reign title by which they were known while on the throne (and many had more than one), and their posthumous temple name. I use the personal names when discussing emperors when they are not on the throne, but otherwise I use their reign names—and follow accepted practice in referring to Han dynasty rulers with the title first (for example, Emperor Han Gaozu) and Ming rulers with the title following the reign name (the Hongwu emperor).

I follow a similar policy when referring to cities. Many Chinese cities have undergone one or more name changes over time, and in general I use the name by which the city was known during the period under consideration (using, for instance, Beijing to refer to China's capital during the modern period, but Dadu or Cambaluc to refer to the city when speaking of Marco Polo's visit during the Yuan). With respect to the nation itself, however, I adopt the opposite solution. Throughout its history, the geographic region corresponding roughly to modern China has been ruled by a variety of (often overlapping) regimes, and has usually been referred to by the name of the dynasty or kingdom controlling the area in question. I will generally use the term *China* to refer to the region throughout the period from the Qin dynasty to the present—with the understanding that this may very well be a strategic anachronism.

One of the central concerns of this volume is the relationship between the conventional perception of the Wall as a singular entity, on one hand, and the wide range of ways in which it has been referred to and understood, on the other. In exploring these issues, I will alternate among a variety of descriptive formulations, such as "the Qin dynasty Wall," "the Ming Wall," "the Long Wall," "the

Barricade," "the Badaling section of the Wall," and even "the Great Wall," to specify different geographical or historical incarnations of the structure, while using the more general term *the Wall* to refer to the monument as an idealized singular and unified structure.

Wherein lies that which makes humanity human?
I say it lies in humanity's possession of boundaries.

—*Xunzi* (third century BCE)

The tenacious wall that at the present moment, and at all
times, projects its system of shadows across lands I will never
see, is precisely the shadow of a Caesar who ordered the most
reverent of nations to burn its past. It is likely that this idea,
aside from the conjectures it might invite, also has the capacity
to affect us in its own right. (The virtue of this idea may lie in its
monumental opposition between processes of construction and
destruction.)

—Jorge Luis Borges, "The Wall and the Books" (1961)

What is then the origin of the Great Wall of China that
circumscribes a "proper" in the text?

—Michel de Certeau, *The Practice of Everyday Life* (1980)

On Origins

Everything must have a start, even a tradition.
—William Edgar Geil, *The Great Wall of China* (1909)

On the final day of President Obama's 2009 trip to China, he was taken on a tour of the Badaling section of the Great Wall just outside Beijing, where he posed for what White House aides celebrated as "the shot." A widely distributed Associated Press photograph depicts the president standing pensively on a rampart, and while we have no way of knowing what precisely he was thinking, the Associated Press's accompanying description offers a hint: "'It's magical,' Mr. Obama said, walking down a ramp alone, his hands in his pockets. 'It reminds you of the sweep of history and our time here on earth is not that long. We better make the best of it.'"[1] Obama's visit to the Wall elicited a brief flurry of excitement in the U.S. news media, but in general it was actually rather unremarkable. A carefully scripted appearance at one of China's most popular tourist destinations, this "shot" rehearses a set of familiar assumptions regarding the Wall's status as a symbol—of historical continuity, of territorial integrity, and of the nation itself.

The apparent familiarity of this scene, however, is belied by a set of suggestive contradictions just beneath the surface. While the

Obama at Badaling. AP Photo/Charles Dharapak (2009).

Wall is often seen as a paradigmatic symbol of China's history, for instance, this particular section has actually been extensively reconstructed in recent years. The Wall is frequently imagined as a quintessential emblem of China's border, yet here it is being used as a scenic backdrop for a visiting foreign leader. And, finally, while the iconic monument is conventionally conceived as a stand-in for the Chinese nation, it is perceived here through coverage by an American news agency. If there is indeed something "magical" about this scene, therefore, it lies in its subtle negotiation of these contradictory connotations of historicity, territorial boundaries, and national identity.

Like Obama's Badaling photo op, the significance of the Wall itself might at first appear to be rather straightforward. The Wall, as every schoolchild knows, represents the nation's power, unity, and longevity. A defensive barricade spanning China's northern frontier and linking contemporary China back to its first unified dynasty, the Wall symbolizes the nation's geographic integrity and historical continuity. It is the longest and most massive structure ever built by man, and the only one visible from outer space.

At the same time, however, it is generally acknowledged that *none* of these claims is strictly accurate. The massive brick and stone Wall we see today was not constructed until around the sixteenth century and is positioned far from the nation's current borders. The structure no longer retains any strategic function as a defensive fortification, and even at the height of its use it often reflected not so much China's strength as its inherent vulnerability. And, no, the Wall is not visible from space—or at least it is no more visible than a number of other man-made structures would be from a comparable distance.

Meanwhile, it has become increasingly conventional to treat the Wall as a set of historically independent structures—differentiating, for instance, between the Ming dynasty's brick-and-stone construction and the tamped-earth structures erected by earlier regimes, such as the Qin dynasty. The problem with this approach, however, is that it opens the door to a potential repudiation of the very notion of the Wall. Once we grant that the Ming and Qin Walls should be treated as physically and historically independent entities, what would prevent us from applying the same logic to, say, the Ming Wall itself—seeing it not as a unified structure but as a set of distinct border-wall constructions carried out under different emperors in different regions over roughly a two-century span? What, indeed, grants *any* wall a unified identity that encompasses the multitude of bricks and stones out of which it is made?

It would, of course, be possible to simply do away with the concept of the Wall and speak instead of geographically and historically specific border-wall construction projects. The problem is, we have a strong *intuition* that the Wall does in fact exist. The challenge, therefore, is to find a way to bring what we know about the structure's empirical history and reality into line with our intuition that it exists as a meaningful entity.

Most contemporary discussions of the Wall approach it as an abstract ideal or a material structure, or a combination of the two. Both the abstract ideal and the material structure, however, are in a continual state of flux, and consequently they do not suffice, in and of themselves, to anchor a vision of the Wall as a historically continuous entity. Instead, the key to the Wall's identity lies in the cultural environment within which it is embedded; this body of cultural representations provides the glue that binds the physically and historically discrete structures into a single unity.

"Even a Tradition"

The Wall, as Obama observed, is often perceived as a symbol of the "sweep of history." To appreciate the significance of the Wall's historical connotations, we may begin by looking beyond the media's representations of Obama's visit to Badaling and consider instead its broader historical context.

On October 1, 2009—approximately a month and a half before Obama's visit—China celebrated with great fanfare the sixtieth anniversary of the People's Republic. This week-long celebration, however, stood in stark contrast to several other anniversaries that year of pivotal moments in modern Chinese history. May Fourth, for instance, was the ninetieth anniversary of the reform movement that marked the transition from imperial to modern China, while March tenth and June Fourth were the fiftieth and twentieth anniversaries, respectively, of antigovernment demonstrations in Tibet and Tiananmen Square that had both been quelled by force. However, while National Day, on October 1, is a major state holiday and May Fourth is commemorated unofficially for its social and cultural significance, the very mention of the 1989 Tiananmen Square crackdown is strictly forbidden and the Tibet Rebellion of 1959 has been recoded as a celebration of China's subsequent "liberation" of the Tibetan serfs. Although each of these four events played an outsize role in helping to shape the culture, society, and politics of modern China, the stark disparity in how their anniversaries are observed illustrates the role of contemporary concerns in shaping a vision of the past.

A similar point may be made about the Wall. Our view of the structure is directly informed by recent attempts to preserve it as a historical monument and to rehabilitate its status as a national icon, among many other factors. Those in other eras have perceived the Wall through their own concerns—seeing it, for instance, through the lens of the First Emperor's legendary tyranny, the Ming dynasty's defensive priorities, or the West's Orientalist fascination with China. While it is true that every period approaches the structure in its own way, it is equally the case that each era's understanding of the structure may itself become part of the Wall's own "future history," informing how subsequent eras come to view the Wall. We may, therefore, regard the Wall as the product of a historical continuity—but in the specific sense of being the product of a continuous process of reinvention.

One hundred years before Obama's trip to Badaling, the American Baptist missionary and amateur adventurer William Edgar Geil published *The Great Wall of China,* in which he speculated that his previous year's trek from one end of the structure to the other "might set in motion among the Chinese a new tradition—everything must have a start, even a tradition—about a wild western man of prodigious height and bulksome weight who traversed the brick of Qin."[2] While Geil's 1909 book on the Wall (the first volume on the subject in any language) is not well known today, his fantasy that he might succeed in "set[ting] in motion . . . a new tradition" succinctly captures an important dimension of the monument's status as a cultural artifact. Over time, countless discourses on the Wall have coalesced into a complex and nuanced tradition. While many of the individual discussions (like Obama's recent remarks and, arguably, even Geil's early book on the subject) may have been comparatively inconsequential in their own right—and often have contained many inaccuracies or outright falsehoods—they each have the potential to contribute to the body of tradition that is the Wall.

New Walls

Obama's visit to Badaling discussed above came on the heels of not only the four China-related anniversaries, but also the twentieth anniversary of the fall of perhaps the ultimate symbol of border barriers in the modern world: the Berlin Wall. Obama himself addressed the significance of the Berlin Wall in a 2008 speech in front of Brandenburg Gate in which he warned that "the greatest danger of all is to allow new walls to divide us from one another." Obama was obviously speaking metaphorically in referring to "new walls," yet he could just as easily have been referring to the proliferation of actual border walls in the contemporary era.

The 1989 fall of the Berlin Wall marked the beginning of the end of the iron curtain, the Eastern bloc, the cold war, and virtually everything else the Berlin Wall had stood for. It did not, however, portend the immediate obsolescence of this sort of barrier. If anything, global enthusiasm for territorial walls and fences has actually increased over the past two decades. Israel, for instance, is constructing a heavily fortified barricade along its internal border with the West Bank, mirroring those it recently built along its border with the Gaza Strip as well as between the Gaza Strip and Egypt. In the mid-1990s, India began constructing a series of barriers along its borders with Bangladesh, Myanmar, and Kashmir, and it is currently contemplating a similar barricade along its border with Pakistan. Iran, meanwhile, has recently begun setting up hundreds of kilometers of fence along its own border with Pakistan, even as Pakistan is proposing to do the same along its border with Afghanistan. China continues to maintain barriers along its borders with

Hong Kong and Macao, even though the former European colonies were returned to Chinese sovereignty in the late 1990s, and in 2006 it began building a new barrier along its border with North Korea (and North Korea has responded with a wall of its own on the other side of the same border). Meanwhile, in 2006 the United States passed the Secure Fence Act, authorizing the "possible" construction of more than 700 miles of a double-layer barrier along the nation's southern border with Mexico—at an estimated cost of billions of dollars.

There is a distinct irony in the fact that, at the turn of the twenty-first century, wealthy and scientifically advanced countries around the world are resorting to comparatively rudimentary technologies of concrete and barbed wire to secure their borders. While these sorts of physical barriers may be effective under certain circumstances, their practical utility is generally limited in the face of the daunting socioeconomic forces that drive movement across international borders, combined with the sheer length of the physical borders themselves. Although the United States has appropriated billions of dollars to erect the series of fortified fences along hundreds of miles of its border with Mexico, for instance, many experts argue that even when complete these barriers will not significantly decrease illegal immigration, but at most will merely shunt attempted border crossings to more remote (and consequently more dangerous) regions. The significance of many of these contemporary walls, therefore, would appear to lie not so much in their status as physical barriers as in their status as abstract symbols of the purposes to which they are ostensibly being put.

China's Wall is haunted by a similar tension between its status as a material artifact and as an abstract ideal. The Wall is frequently imagined as an unthinkably massive barrier, yet the material structure itself no longer retains any strategic function, and even at its peak effectiveness its significance often lay more in its status as a *symbol* of the border than as an actual barricade. We could, there-

Obama at Badaling, with "One World One Dream" sign in background.
AP Photo/Andy Wong (2009).

fore, see the Wall as a material barrier, but one whose materiality is often symbolic in nature.

One World

On the mountainside directly behind the Badaling section of the Wall there is a large sign with the English-language phrase, "One World One Dream." Echoing the title of the 1985 charity anthem "We Are the World" (with which a People's Liberation Army band had hilariously serenaded Obama at a state dinner the night before his Badaling visit), One World One Dream was the official motto of the 2008 Beijing Olympics. This seemingly straightforward slogan, however, is actually grounded on a peculiar tension, balanced between parallel appeals to cosmopolitan consensus and national distinctiveness.

Beijing's Olympic committee claimed that the One World One Dream motto was a composite of nearly a quarter of a million suggested wordings the committee had received from around the world. Underlying this facade of global consensus, however, is a strategic ambiguity at the heart of the slogan, in that it pointedly leaves unstated what the nature of this "dream" is that the world is imagined to be sharing. The motto's rhetorical echo of China's contemporary One China principle suggests, for instance, that the slogan's underlying logic could be interpreted as: One World One Dream . . . One China. The international protests that persistently dogged Beijing's preparations for the Olympic Games, meanwhile, suggest a rather different reading that was made explicit when a group of international protesters rappelled down the Mutianyu section of the Wall near Beijing in July 2007 with a banner that read "One World, One Dream, Free Tibet 2008."

Just as the appeal of the One World motto lies in its strategic ambiguity, the Wall's status as a globally recognized symbol of China is predicated on its ability to permit a range of interpretations while appearing to present a unified front. The Wall's power as a national icon, in other words, is made possible by the protean transformations of its representations as they circulate throughout China and beyond.

Citation

Upon concluding his Badaling photo shoot, Obama reportedly followed up his "sweep of history" remarks with an unscripted aside: "I also think I'm glad I didn't carry a camera." The president was presumably expressing his relief at not having to hold a camera on that bitterly cold day, but his remark could also be seen as a comment on the impossibility of ever being able to capture an accurate representation of the Wall.

For everyone other than the small group of officials and reporters who accompanied Obama to Badaling, perception of the Badaling photo op is necessarily mediated through representations offered by the Associated Press and other news agencies. Some of the limits of this media filter can be seen when one considers a rough, forty-six-second video clip recorded at the time, in which Obama strolls casually down the rampart, then pauses and remarks, "It's majestic. It's a reminder of the incredible history of the Chinese people. And I think it gives you a good perspective on the fact that a lot of the day-to-day things we worry about don't amount to much compared to the sweep of history."[3] This clip records the same moment seen in Charles Dharapak's photograph and features the same comments quoted in AP bureau chief Charles Hutzler's accompanying article, while presenting a distinctly different view of the scene itself. The point here, however, is not to contrast the objectivity of the video clip with the distortions that characterize the newspaper coverage (though with respect to the precise wording of Obama's statement, the video is obviously more reliable), but to emphasize that *all* representations are shaped by their own specific perspective (including such seemingly minor details as the angle of a shot and how it is framed).

The AP's coverage of Obama's Badaling shot circulated throughout the world, and also inspired a variety of secondary representations. Hutzler's "paraquote" of Obama's comments was not only picked up by syndicated media services, for instance, but was also cited (often without attribution) in a range of other sources, including an article in the English-language edition of China's official newspaper, *The People's Daily*.[4] Dharapak's photograph also circulated widely, and was appropriated a few months later for an ad on a Times Square billboard for the apparel company Weatherproof, which had made the jacket Obama happened to be wearing during the visit (the company quickly agreed to take down the ad after the White House protested its use of the president's image).

At first glance, *The People's Daily*'s unattributed citation of the AP's paraquote of Obama's comments and Weatherproof's unau-

Times Square billboard showing Obama at Badaling.
AP Photo/Julie Jacobson (2010).

thorized appropriation of the AP's carefully framed photograph of the scene might appear to constitute second-order betrayals of the "reality" of the original scene (which, needless to say, was a carefully staged fiction to begin with). From a different perspective, however, these processes of citation and appropriation illustrate in miniature the cultural logic that underlies the Wall itself. The contemporary Wall is a product of a continual process of citation, as each era cites and adapts different discursive elements it has inherited from earlier periods. It is precisely in the resulting *cultural incarnation* of the Wall—rather than in its status as a singular ideal or a unitary structure—that we find the key to its identity. It is here, in other words, that we find the secret to the Great Wall's greatness.

What follows, accordingly, is a *cultural* history of the Wall. My primary focus is neither on the structure's concrete materiality nor on its empirical historicity as such, but rather on a multifaceted body of cultural representations of the monument. These representations have not only shaped the ways in which the Wall has been understood throughout its history but have even played a direct role in driving the repeated construction (and reconstruction) of the actual structure. These cultural representations, in other words, quite literally *are* the Wall, and without them the monument as we know it would be unthinkable.

CHAPTER 1

A Unity of Gaps

In this way, the system of piecemeal construction makes sense . . .
and as inconsequential as it might first appear, this is actually a
central question relating to the entire construction of the Wall.

—Franz Kafka, "The Great Wall of China" (1917)

A structure of notoriously vast proportions, the Wall is frequently
cited as a symbol par excellence for entities whose enormity boggles
the mind. For instance, the Chinese basketball player Yao Ming—
who, at seven feet six inches, is currently the tallest player in the
NBA—is nicknamed China's Great Wall. When Yao Ming teams
up with his compatriots, the seven-foot-one Wang Zhizhi and the
six-foot-eleven Menk Batere from Inner Mongolia—as he did for
the 2000 Summer Olympics in Sydney and the 2001 Pan-Asian
Games—the trio is referred to as China's Walking Great Wall. Even
the giant Yao Ming, however, is dwarfed by a celestial Great Wall,
officially known as the CfA2 Great Wall: a sheet of galaxies 500
million light years across that was the largest known structure in
the universe when it was discovered in 1989. The CfA2 Great Wall
didn't hold that distinction long, however, as four years later astronomers using data from the Sloan Digital Sky Survey discovered
another, even greater, "Great Wall." Dubbed the Sloan Great Wall,
this galaxy supercluster is estimated to be 1.37 billion light years

13

across and, for the moment at least, holds the title of largest entity known to man.

Able to inspire these sorts of larger-than-life comparisons, the Great Wall itself is undeniably great. "Great," that is, both in the colloquial sense of being amazing and awe inspiring and also in the more specific meaning of the term that Kant invokes in his *Critique of Judgment:* "We call that sublime which is absolutely great."[1] For Kant, the mathematical sublime is an aesthetic category corresponding to that which inspires a sense of fear precisely because it lies beyond the limits of human understanding. The sublime is characterized, Kant argues, by its quality of "boundlessness," even as the *category* of the sublime itself is necessarily bounded within the realm of the aesthetic. A viewer of a painting of an immense mountain, for instance, may well feel a sense of awe and fear—but this sublime reaction is nevertheless very different from the genuine terror a traveler would feel if he were to find himself precariously perched on the pinnacle of that same mountain.

If we accept Kant's definition of the sublime, the Wall is indeed great by virtue of its sublimity. It is the quintessential symbol of territorial, ethnic, and historical boundaries, but at the same time it exemplifies the quality Kant calls "boundlessness." Stretching across thousands of kilometers of northern China, extending thousands of years into the nation's past, and constructed by untold millions of now-anonymous laborers, the Wall exists on a scale almost beyond our comprehension. And yet, part of the landmark's contemporary appeal lies in the fact that it appears so eminently comprehensible. The Wall, in other words, functions as an accessible fragment of the infinite—an easily intelligible symbol of that which, by its very nature, virtually defies human understanding.

This aspect of the Wall's sublimity is manifested in a long-standing fascination with the structure's length. The standard term for the Wall in contemporary Chinese is *chang cheng,* which means "long wall" or "long walls" and was used as early as the Warring

States period to designate the territorial border walls constructed by the rival kingdoms in China's Central Plains. A more formal version of the term—one that is derived from the Han historian Sima Qian's famous description, in his seminal work, *Records of the Historian,* of the border fortifications the Qin dynasty's first emperor constructed across the northern border of his newly unified territory—adds an element of precision to this characterization by specifying that the structure was a *wanli chang cheng,* or, literally, a "ten-thousand-*li*-long long wall." A *li* is a traditional Chinese unit of length that under the Qin dynasty's historic standardization of weights and measures was assigned a value equivalent to slightly more than five hundred meters (roughly a third of a mile), though the Qin's successor, the Han dynasty, recalibrated the number of *chi* (Chinese feet) in a *li* and decreased the length of the *li* by one-sixth. In any event, the precise length of the *li* in Sima Qian's description of a "ten-thousand-*li*-long long wall" is ultimately irrelevant, given that this was at best a rough approximation of the structure's size. In fact, it has often been argued that Sima Qian was using *wan* (ten thousand) not as a precise number but rather in the general sense of "myriad," and was using *li* not as a specific unit of length but rather as a mere metaphor for length.

Not satisfied with Sima Qian's highly approximate—and arguably formulaic—estimate of the Wall's length, generations of visitors have struggled to come to terms with the structure's immensity by attempting to quantify its dimensions as precisely as possible. When Lord Macartney led the first British embassy to China in 1793, for instance, he and his companions were escorted to the Gubeikou section of the Wall about one hundred kilometers northeast of Beijing, where several of them made extensive measurements of the structure they found there. Macartney's private secretary, the accountant and one-time mathematics instructor John Barrow, later used Macartney's measurements to calculate its overall size, writing that the Wall is so enormous, that admitting, what I believe has never been denied, its length to be fifteen hundred miles, and the dimensions throughout pretty much the same as where it was crossed by the British Embassy, the materials of all the dwelling-houses of England and Scotland, supposing them to amount to 1,800,000, and to average on the whole 2,000 cubic feet of masonry or brick-work, are barely equivalent to the bulk or solid contents of the Great Wall of China. Nor are the projecting massy towers of stone and brick included in this calculation. These alone, supposing them to continue throughout at bow-shot distance, were calculated to contain as much masonry and brickwork as all London. To give another idea of the mass of matter in this stupendous fabric, it may be observed, that it is more than sufficient to surround the circumference of the earth on two of its great circles, with two walls, each six feet high and two feet thick![2]

While there is obviously no disputing the Wall's immense size, it is nevertheless telling that Barrow's elaborate calculations were based on an extrapolation from the finite section of the structure that he happened to visit in person. The former mathematician was, in other words, using an exhaustive measurement of the section at hand in an attempt to quantify the dimensions of a structure that seemed to stretch to the limits of the human imagination.

Even today, almost all discussions of the Wall include an obligatory specification of its length, as if the act of assigning the structure a number (any number, really) might somehow render it more comprehensible. The range of these figures, however, underscores just how limited our knowledge of the Wall really is. China's official Xinhua News Service, for instance, has cited lengths ranging from a modest 3,000 kilometers to more than 60,000 (with the second estimate referring not simply to the Wall's linear trajectory, but rather to the sum of all of the [mutually overlapping] individual border walls constructed throughout this region). While one might think that the question of the Wall's length could be put to rest by a comprehensive survey of the structure, the first such survey was not begun until 2007. In 2009, authorities announced they had finished the measurement of the Ming Wall, but that they wouldn't finish surveying the surviving fragments of earlier long walls until 2011. As ambitious and methodical as this survey may be, it will not definitively resolve the matter of the structure's dimensions—for the simple reason that asking *how long* the Wall is inevitably begs the question of *what* it is. Which structures are considered part of the Wall, and how intact do they have to be to be considered extant? What are the structural limits of the physical wall, and what is its relationship to the natural barriers that were integrated into its construction?

The question of the Wall's length is ultimately unanswerable because it is an ontological issue masquerading as an epistemological one—an attempt to use quantitative measures to address a problem that is inherently conceptual and even existential. The absurdities of the contemporary obsession with the Wall's precise dimensions are dramatically illustrated in a recent book by Jing Ai, an archaeologist from the Chinese Academy of Cultural Relics. Jing concludes his volume with a discussion of the Wall's length, noting that,

> due to differences in measuring methodologies, a range of figures has been cited for the lengths of China's historical long walls, and consequently there are wide disparities in the estimates of the Wall's overall length. Some journals and books claim that the Wall is one hundred thousand *li* long, which is to say fifty thousand kilometers. This is a very imprecise approximation that exaggerates the Wall's true length. The question of the Wall's length is of utmost importance, given that it provides the foundation for the implementation of China's Wall-preservation plans. It is, therefore, necessary to establish the length of the Wall as accurately and reliably as possible.[3]

Jing Ai responds to the frustration with the imprecision of existing approximations of the Wall's length by providing a detailed calculation of the Wall's length based not on geological and archaeological surveys of the contemporary monument, but on a detailed analysis of historical accounts of its component structures. After adding together the lengths of each of these individual walls, he comes up with a total of 34,107.53 kilometers of Wall. He then slashes off 12,959.60 kilometers to avoid double-counting overlapping sections of the Wall from different periods, arriving at a total of 21,147.93 kilometers. The problem with these hilariously precise sums is that they are derived from historical texts that typically provide, as Jing himself openly admits, figures that are at best rough approximations. Whereas many of the pre-Ming texts cite lengths consisting of only one or two significant digits (as is true of Sima Qian's famous characterization of the Qin Wall as "stretching over a distance of more than ten thousand *li*"), Jing nevertheless combines these approximations with the much more precise Ming dynasty measurements to yield a final sum that specifies the Wall's total length down to the nearest centimeter.

As if troubled by the yawning disparity between the extraordinary precision of his extrapolated lengths and the highly approximate nature of the historical measurements on which he draws, Jing supplements his analysis with a discussion of the shifting values of traditional Chinese units of length, from the nation's first unified dynasty, the Qin, up to its final dynasty, the Qing. Oddly, though, he focuses not on the *li* (Chinese mile) itself but on the length of the much shorter *chi* (Chinese foot)—as if knowing that during the Qin dynasty a *chi* was (according to Jing) 23.1 centimeters long, while by the Qing dynasty 2,000 years later it had increased by 38.5 percent to 32.0 centimeters, might somehow give greater authenticity to Sima Qian's characterization of the Qin dynasty Wall as being ten thousand *li* long. Even in this discussion, the sheer hyperbole of Jing's precision appears to suggest an anxiety about the rationale behind the attempt to concretize the length of the Wall—and, specifically, a tension between a desire to regard the structure as a unitary entity and an awareness of its inherent heterogeneity.

A similar tension between unity and heterogeneity can be found in the Wall's current iconic status. The Wall is prominently featured on China's currency and its foreign visas, in its national anthem, and even in a huge tapestry China presented to the United Nations, though each of these representations also carries a cluster of competing connotations that simultaneously undercut the monument's ostensible nationalistic significance. The image of the Wall on China's one-yuan bills, for instance, serves as a reminder of the pervasive commoditization—and, some would argue, the attendant trivialization—of the icon, while its inclusion on China's foreign visas suggests its current role, not in keeping foreigners *out* of China but in helping shepherd them *in*. The prominent allusion to the Wall in the national anthem brings into relief the lyrics' curious omission of any explicit reference to Maoism, just as the tapestry presented to the UN upon China's admission in 1971 symbolically papers over the political chasm between the People's Republic of China (PRC) and the Republic of China (ROC), also known as Taiwan, which had held the "China" seat on the United Nations Security Council since the organization was founded in 1945. Like any good national symbol, therefore, the Wall is not so much a straightforward emblem of an idealized vision of the nation as it is a vivid reminder of the processes of fragmentation that invariably underlie our perception of China as a unified and unitary entity.

This perception of the Wall as simultaneously unified and fractured—and also as a symbol of both unity and fragmentation—informs our vision of the material structure. "The Great Wall's greatness lies in its totality," the British Wall enthusiast William Lindesay recently affirmed. "If there's one brick less, or another gap to make way for a dirt road, then the continuity of the wall is broken and its value is reduced."[4] A distance runner who spent several months in 1987 attempting to jog the entire length of the Wall, Lindesay was struck by how much of the structure he found to be in ruins or even missing altogether. He subsequently went on to establish an international organization called Friends of the Great Wall, which has been instrumental in spearheading efforts to protect the historic monument from the combined forces of erosion, vandalism, and sloppy restoration. However, underlying the practical efforts to prevent further destruction of the historic monument and restore the portions that have survived, there is the unstated question of what sort of "totality" the Wall is in the first place. Lindesay contends that the Wall is threatened by a variety of forces that compromise the structure's integrity, but what if it was never an integral and continuous structure to begin with? What if its physical "continuity," in other words, was from the very beginning already "broken"?

A fascinating engagement with this question of the Wall's alleged totality may be found in an explosion event entitled *Project to Extend the Great Wall by 10,000 Meters: Project for Extraterrestrials No. 10*, by the Chinese-born artist Cai Guo-Qiang. On February 27, 1993, Cai, whose artistic media of choice include pyrotechnics, prepared a ten-kilometer line of bags of gunpowder spaced at three-meter intervals, beginning at the Jiayuguan fort at the westernmost end of the Wall and stretching out from there, deep into the desert. Just before dusk he lit a fuse at the Wall end of the line of explosives, triggering a chain of detonations that raced across the desert toward the distant mountains. The result was a virtual Wall, created out of a spectacle of its own virtual destruction.

Cai's medium for this work is revealing. Gunpowder is a quintessential symbol not only of physical destruction but also of China's own heritage. Gunpowder is thought to have been invented in Tang dynasty China, and in using it here, Cai—whose given name, Guo-Qiang, means "strong nation"—employs a spectacularly destruc-

Cai Guo-Qiang (b. 1957, Quanzhou, China; lives in New York), preparations for *Project to Extend the Great Wall of China by 10,000 Meters: Project for Extraterrestrials No. 10,* 1993. Realized at the Gobi Desert, west of the Great Wall, Jiayuguan, Gansu Province, February 27, 1993, 7:35 PM, 15 minutes. Explosion length: 10,000 meters; gunpowder (600 kg) and two fuse lines (10,000 m each). Commissioned by P3 art and environment, Tokyo.

Photo by Masanobu Moriyama, courtesy Cai Studio.

tive medium to recreate a vision of one of China's most recognizable symbols.

Although it has been claimed that approximately 40,000 people came to observe Cai Guo-Qiang's explosion event in remote Gansu Province (a spectacularly high number, given that the population of the city of Jiayuguan is only around 100,000), the artist's "ideal" audience can perhaps be inferred from the title of the series in which *Extend the Great Wall* was his tenth installment: Project for Extraterrestrials. This series has included works such as Cai's 1992 performance *Fetus Movement II* (in which he positioned himself at the center of a series of concentric circles of gunpowder that he then detonated while keeping detailed visual and audio records of his own brain and cardiac activity), and each of these performances combines elements of extreme intimacy and sublime monumentality to convey an experience that transcends our human senses and attempts to interrogate the very conditions of vision itself.

Of the various works in Cai's Project for Extraterrestrials series, it was his *Project to Extend the Great Wall by 10,000 Meters* explosion event that engaged most evocatively with the perceptual concerns implicit in the series' title, given that the Wall has itself long been haunted by a fantasy of extraterrestrial perception. In view of the Wall's vast physical and historical dimensions, visitors must approach it in a piecemeal fashion and then attempt to extrapolate the entirety of the Wall from the isolated fragments they happen to see before them. The resulting tension between the visitors' actual view of the Wall as inherently fragmentary and their idealized vision of the structure as a unitary entity, is articulated most clearly in the old chestnut about the Wall's being the only manmade structure visible to the naked eye from space—from Earth orbit, from the moon, or even from Mars.

Needless to say, the claims about the Wall's extraterrestrial visibility are either absurd or, at best, meaningless. No terrestrial manmade structure is remotely visible to the naked eye from the moon; even from a low Earth orbit, only objects at least several hundred meters across (along their narrowest axis, as viewed from overhead) have any hope of being glimpsed without artificial magnification. The Wall's immense length is essentially irrelevant here, given that the limiting factor would necessarily be the structure's relatively narrow width, which rarely exceeds six or seven meters (somewhat more if the Wall's own shadow is factored in). To put this into perspective, seeing the Wall from even a 160-kilometer orbit would be equivalent to discerning a two-centimeter-wide ribbon from more than half a kilometer away. Even if this were possible (and it's not, given the physiological limits of human vision), the claim that the Wall is one of the only man-made objects visible from space—if not *the* only object—would remain nonsensical because there are countless other structures whose narrowest dimensions vastly exceed the Wall's width, and that consequently would be significantly more visible from any comparable distance.

Despite its patent implausibility, the visible-from-space fantasy has enjoyed a surprisingly resilient hold on the popular imagination. Versions of the claim can be found everywhere from Western academic publications to Chinese elementary school textbooks, and even professional astronauts have debated among themselves whether or not they were able to see the Wall during their voyages. Neil Armstrong, for instance, notes in an interview that he had "not yet found somebody who has told me they've seen the Wall of China from Earth orbit. I'm not going to say there aren't people, but I personally haven't talked to them. I've asked various people, particularly Shuttle guys, that have been [on] many orbits around China in the daytime, and the ones I've talked to didn't see it."[5] In 2003 the first Chinese astronaut in space, Yang Liwei, precipitated a national crisis when he reported that he had not been able to glimpse the Wall during his twenty-one and a half hours in orbit (thereby prompting China's Ministry of Education to request that a publisher remove the "visible from space" claim from elementary school textbooks). More recently, the Chinese-American astronaut Leroy Chiao apparently did succeed in capturing a faint image of the Wall in a photograph taken from the International Space Station, but only with the aid of a powerful telephoto lens. As fellow Chinese-American astronaut Ed Lu has said, the Wall is indeed visible from space under ideal conditions (ones, however, that necessarily include considerable artificial magnification), though "it's less visible than a lot of other objects. And you have to know where to look."[6]

The most influential popularizer of the visible-from-space claim was Robert Ripley (who was apparently so fond of China that he once remarked, "If I could be reincarnated, I'd return as a Chinese").[7] In a 1932 *Believe It or Not!* cartoon panel, he described the Wall as "the mightiest work of man—the only one that would be visible to the human eye from the moon."[8] Such was the allure of this claim that even Joseph Needham, the influential historian of science and technology in China, made a tongue-in-cheek allusion to it when he dryly observed that the Wall "has been considered the only work of man which could be picked out by Martian astronomers."[9] This fascination with the possibility of viewing the Wall from space can be traced back to long before space travel was even a remote possibility. As early as 1754, for instance, the English antiquary William Stukeley described Hadrian's Wall in Britain as a "mighty wall of four score miles in length [that] is only exceeded by the Chinese wall, which makes a considerable figure upon the terrestrial globe, and may be discerned at the moon."[10]

In 1781, Edward Gibbon described the Wall as a "stupendous work, which holds a conspicuous place in the map of the world," and indeed the origins of the fantasy of the Wall's extraterrestrial visibility may be traced back to a cartographic tradition dating almost to the beginning of the second millennium.[11] We find an iconic image of a crenellated Wall on the earliest map of China to appear in a Western atlas, Abraham Ortelius and Luis Jorge de Barbuda's 1584 *Chinae, olim sinarum regionis, nova descriptio,* on which the Wall—interspersed with stretches of mountains—appears in red along the right side of the westward-oriented map. More than four hundred years earlier, a Chinese map entitled *A Geographic Map* in a Chinese encyclopedia—said to be the oldest extant printed map in the world—also clearly depicts the Wall stretching across China's northern frontier. While the Ortelius and Barbuda map also features a number of other icons, of ships, wagons, castles, and so on, on this earlier, Southern Song map, the Wall depicted at the top is

"The Great Wall of China," Robert Ripley, *Believe It or Not!* (1932).
Copyright © 2009 Ripley Entertainment, Inc.

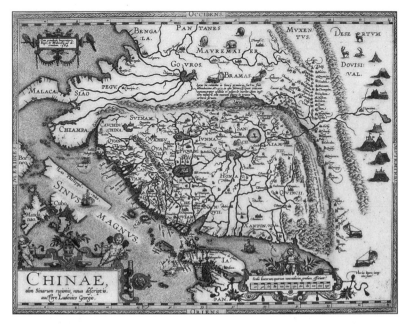

Chinae, olim sinarum regionis, nova descriptio: Auctore Ludouico Georgio, Abraham Ortelius and Luis Jorge de Barbuda (1584).
Courtesy of the Hong Kong University of Science and Technology.

the *only* man-made structure represented—which is particularly notable given that it is a representation not of a structure in existence at the time, but of a cultural memory of the no-longer extant Qin dynasty Wall.

Why *has* this obsession with the Wall's extraterrestrial visibility taken such a resilient hold on the popular imagination? The reason, I would suggest, for the persistent appeal of this notion is that our idealized *vision* of the Wall persistently exceeds our actual *view* of the structure itself. Despite the Wall's status as one of the world's best-known symbols of terrestrial borders, the fascination with the possibility of seeing it from an extraterrestrial perspective reflects an underlying fantasy of being able to transcend those same borders.

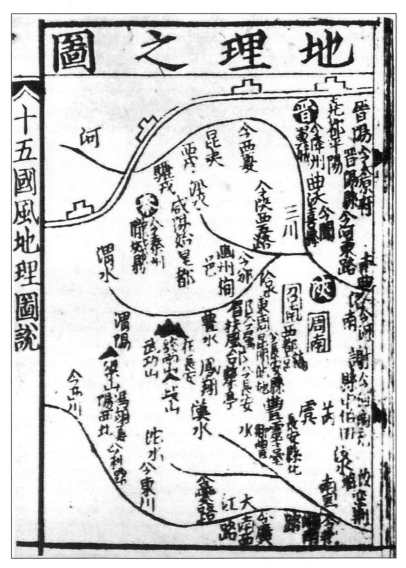

A Geographic Map [Dili zhitu], Southern Song map of northwestern China (1155).

Reprinted with the permission of Cambridge University Press.

We might, therefore, take this conceit at face value and ask what *would* the Wall look like glimpsed from an Archimedean position radically outside these specific national and cultural discourses— from the perspective, say, of Needham's proverbial Martian astronomers? The beginning of an answer may be found in a famous thought experiment proposed by the Harvard philosopher W. V. O. Quine to illustrate the indeterminacy of translation. Imagine, Quine suggests, a linguist visiting an unfamiliar tribe. When a rabbit runs past, a native points to it and says, "*Gavagai.*" Would the linguist be correct in assuming that *gavagai* means the same thing as our concept of rabbit? The answer necessarily depends, Quine argues, on the native's assumptions about identity and reference. It is entirely possible that, rather than denoting a temporally continuous and physically unified organism, as we do with *rabbit,* the native might be conceptually carving up the world very differently from the way we do. He might, for instance, be referring to such (apparent) metaphysical oddities as an isolated temporal slice of rabbit, an assemblage of undetached rabbit parts, an abstract fusion of all rabbits, or even the recurrent universal of "rabbithood." Or, alternatively, we could extend Quine's point by suggesting that the native might indeed be using *gavagai* to denote a member of a category of continuous and unified organisms, yet positioning that category within a taxonomical system completely different from our own.[12]

Borrowing from Jorge Luis Borges's imaginary "Chinese encyclopedia"—a text in which the animal kingdom is divided into categories so exotic that they famously provoked Michel Foucault to an uproarious "laughter that shattered . . . all the landmarks of my thought," and led him to marvel at "the exotic charm of another system of thought" and its ability to point to the "limitation of our own, the stark impossibility of thinking *that*"—we might speculate that Quine's native could have been positioning his concept of the *gavagai* within such seemingly bizarre categories as "[animals] that belong to the emperor," "those that from a long way off look like flies," or even "those included in the present classification."[13] We tend to assume that our understanding of the world is the only one possible—or at least the most intuitive one—but in fact ours is just one of a vast number of equally plausible ways of conceptually carving up reality and classifying its contents.

In any of these Quinean or Borgesian scenarios, the difficulty lies not so much in identifying the concrete referent of the word *gavagai* (that is, the animal at which the native is pointing when he utters the word) but in deciphering the underlying *meaning* of the term (the significance of the term in the native's own mind). Without a detailed discussion of their respective taxonomical and metaphysical assumptions, however, it is entirely possible that neither the linguist nor the native would realize that they might well be talking about completely different things. A similar point can be made with respect to the meaning and significance of the Wall. If one of Needham's imaginary Martian astronomers were to observe an earthling pointing at the Wall and uttering the words *Great Wall,* would the Martian necessarily assume the phrase denotes a unitary, transhistorical entity, or might it instead take it to mean something entirely different—perhaps a specific segment of the Wall, a discrete temporal slice of the Wall, the abstract fusion of segments of the Wall, or the recurrent universal of Wallness? Would the extraterrestrial observer necessarily assume that the referent of the term *Great Wall* belongs to a general category of territorial border walls, or might it instead understand the term in the context of a more esoteric conceptual system, one consisting, for example, of such categories as "those walls built by the emperor," "those walls one imagines can be seen from outer space," or even "those walls included under the present classification"? Then again, perhaps the Martian would assume that the term *Great Wall* means something different altogether, something so alien to our own way of thinking that we might not even have the vocabulary with which to describe it.

The flip side to speculating about imaginary extraterrestrials would be asking how *we ourselves* perceive the Wall. Are we confident about our own understanding of terms like *Great Wall* and *chang cheng,* and can we ever be certain that others understand them the same way we do? Actually, we don't need to appeal to imaginary Martian astronomers or other extraterrestrials to appreciate some of the practical consequences of the issues Quine raises. We may consider, for instance, a recent book in which William Lindesay juxtaposes photographs of the Wall from the turn of the twentieth century with more recent ones he himself took from almost precisely the same locations. The book is designed to illustrate the extent of the Wall's deterioration over the past century, but in doing this it presupposes what Lindesay himself might call the "[historical] continuity of the Wall." When we see, say, John Thomson's historic 1871 photograph of Badaling, how do we know for certain that we are seeing part of a temporally continuous structure that has existed for hundreds (if not thousands) of years, as opposed to merely an isolated temporal slice of Wall? The problem is that a photograph necessarily captures only a spatially distinct and temporally discrete slice of reality, and to make sense of the image we must first make certain assumptions about what lies beyond the frame of the photograph. It is in the invisible margins of the image that the subject of the photograph truly comes to life, endowed with the metaphysical underpinnings that allow us to conceive of it as a coherent entity.

To take an even more concrete example, we could make a similar Quinean point about the inherent indeterminacy of the conventional Chinese term for the Wall: *chang cheng* (long walls). This term was used as early as the fifth century BCE to describe border walls built by the various Central Plains kingdoms to defend themselves from their pastoral-nomadic neighbors to the north, as well as from each other. While it is true that some of these early walls are regarded as the conceptual or even physical antecedents of what we now know as the Great Wall, technically speaking the term *chang cheng* initially functioned not as a proper name referring to a singular Wall, but rather as a descriptive phrase describing a general category of territorial border walls. In fact, given that Chinese generally does not distinguish orthographically between proper and common nouns, or even between singular and plural ones, the term *chang cheng* could—from a strictly lexical and syntactic perspective—refer to a specific entity, a general category of objects, or even a multitude of unrelated structures. We can, therefore, easily imagine two people—one of them in the present and the other in the distant past—standing in the same location along the Wall, pointing to different incarnations of the same structure and uttering the *same word* (after allowing for the phonetic drift of the Chinese language), yet understanding the term in very different ways.

This question of the relationship among the Wall's name, its meaning, and its physical referent is further complicated by the fact that *chang cheng* is only one of many terms that historically have been used to refer to the structure, with others including *guo* (fortification or outer city wall), *yuan* (embankment), *zhang* (barrier), and *sai* (barricade or frontier). When the stone Wall we see today was being constructed around the sixteenth century, the Ming court made a point of *not* referring to it as a *chang cheng*, presumably to avoid the negative associations of the Qin dynasty term, and instead called its new walls *bianqiang* (border walls) or *jiu bianzhen* (nine border garrisons). Many of the terms that have been used to refer to the Wall also have more general meanings. *Guo, yuan,* and *zhang* can all be used as common nouns referring to fortifications and the like. Even the *cheng* in *chang cheng* was borrowed from a general term meaning wall or rampart that may also be used more specifically to refer to city walls, or to cities themselves.

The historian Arthur Waldron argues that the sheer range of

terms that have been used to refer to what we now regard as the Wall is evidence that there must never have been a singular "Great Wall" to begin with:

> [If] an ancient Great Wall had existed, *it almost certainly would have had a single, fixed name,* just as mountains, rivers, temples, etc. do, which would have been used consistently. When dynasties restored or repaired that Wall, as we are told they did, they would have used that name. Yet when we turn to the vocabulary used by Chinese to describe wall-building, we find not a single name, but rather a range of terms and usages that are utterly inconsistent with such a situation.
>
> . . .
>
> If the Ming had been repairing an ancient and well-known "Great Wall," it seems likely that they *would have had little choice but to continue to use its traditional name.* Apparently no word or phrase in the traditional Chinese lexicon corresponds exactly to the modern Western term "Great Wall."[14]

This point about the multiplicity of names used to refer to the Wall is one of the capstones of Waldron's argument that the Wall as we now know it is basically a modern invention. His logic, however, is fundamentally flawed. Although it is certainly legitimate to ask whether different utterances of a particular term or phrase necessarily refer to the same physical and conceptual entity, it is nevertheless rather odd to claim that when the Ming was building its new border wall, it "would have had little choice" but to use an earlier name, had one existed.

In fact, it is actually quite common for buildings, cities, countries, and even people to be assigned new names—even when they already have perfectly good ones—while maintaining a continuous identity. When China temporarily relocated its capital to Nanjing at the beginning of the Ming, and again at the beginning of the twentieth century, for instance, the city currently known as Beijing (literally, northern capital) was briefly renamed Beiping (north pacified). When the Ming court moved the capital back north in 1421, it rebuilt the city that the preceding Yuan dynasty had used for *its* capital (during which time it was known in Mongolian as Khanbaliq, or great residence of the khan, and in Chinese as Dadu, or great capital) and restored its former name of Beijing, as it had been known during the Jin dynasty. Through these multiple name changes, the city is nevertheless perceived as having enjoyed a continuous existence. By a similar logic, one can view the Wall as a coherent entity despite having been referred to by a variety of different names over the course of its existence.

Implicit in the question of how we refer to the Wall is the more general issue of how names denote their referents. One theoretical model advanced at the turn of the twentieth century by the philosopher and mathematician Gottlob Frege, for instance, posits that the "sense" or meaning of a proper name (as opposed to its physical referent) is determined by the cluster of attributes with which it is associated in the mind of the speaker. *William Shakespeare,* for instance, would be shorthand for a nugget of information along the lines of: the seventeenth-century playwright whose works include *Hamlet, King Lear,* et cetera, and who is known as William Shakespeare. Another model developed in the early twentieth century by Bertrand Russell contends that the meaning of a proper name is determined by a chain of reference connecting the name to its referent. An utterance of the name William Shakespeare, by this logic, is anchored to its referent by a series of citations linking the name back to the bard's original baptism. The stakes of this debate become apparent if we imagine a counterfactual scenario in which virtually everything we *think* we know about someone or something is discovered to be erroneous. If it were to be proven that all of the works published under Shakespeare's name had actually been written by, say, Sir Francis Bacon, we might then need to reevaluate our understanding of the name Shakespeare. Would the name William Shakespeare, under this scenario, continue to refer to the individual who originally went by that name, or would it refer instead to Bacon—on the grounds that the latter would now best match the qualities we associate with the name Shakespeare?

The current consensus is that we use proper names not "descriptively," to denote clusters of attributes, but "anti-descriptively," to denote concrete referents that are linked to the names by direct chains of reference. The problem, however, is that this consensus reflects the culturally specific intuitions we happen to have regarding how denotation works, rather than an intrinsic characteristic of proper names themselves. A recent experiment, for instance, presented English-speaking college students from Hong Kong and the United States with a version of the hypothetical Shakespeare/Bacon scenario described above, and concluded that the Hong Kong students were significantly more likely to reach "descriptivist" conclusions than were the Americans—suggesting that there is in fact a sociocultural dimension to our intuitions of how naming and reference work.[15] Though perhaps inconclusive, this experiment suggests that "our" anti-descriptivist intuitions are themselves the product of a descriptivist logic—in that they are not directly grounded in a stable external referent, but reflect a cluster of culturally specific assumptions that happen to prevail at the current moment.

Applying the terms of these philosophy-of-language debates to the Wall, we may ask what is the relationship between the names for the Wall and their referents or meanings? Is the meaning of each name determined strictly by the cluster of attributes associated with it at any particular historical moment, or is it instead directly grounded in the material structure itself? A descriptivist would conclude that our notion of "the Wall" is actually a recent invention, and to the extent that other names historically used to refer to the Wall have carried different sets of associations, they must therefore have different meanings. An anti-descriptivist presumably would

not be overly troubled by these historical shifts in the way the structure has been understood, so long as the underlying continuity and
coherence of the Wall's identity continues to be secured by an unbroken chain of reference linking each usage back to the actual referent.

This chain-of-reference metaphor, however, is ultimately just
that, a metaphor, and as such it is only as strong as its weakest link.
In particular, any two utterances of a name are necessarily separated by a temporal gap, and determining whether the "link" between these citations is strictly causal or merely casual requires that
we fill in this figurative gap with a narrative of some sort. The question of how and whether a name matches its referent ultimately depends on the stories we tell ourselves to explain the relations between names and objects. Furthermore, this process of constructing
a narrative to link a name back to its material referent mirrors
our attempts to connect a specific portion of the Wall to our abstract vision of it as a unitary structure. All but the most naive and
ahistorical views of the monument recognize that it is in fact *not* a
single continuous and physically unified entity, and instead is comprised of a set of independent fragments that are often not even
physically connected to the other fragments that historically preceded them. To make the jump from a discrete Wall fragment to a
notion of a larger, unitary structure, therefore, requires a leap of
faith—the postulation of some sort of story to fill in the various
physical gaps and historical interregnums that stand between us
and a vision of the Wall's totality.

One of the most eloquent commentaries on the Wall's structural
incompleteness may be found in a parable Franz Kafka wrote in
1917 as the Great War was ripping Europe asunder, in which he
discusses the role of the Great Wall in helping to bring the Chinese
empire together. Kafka's narrator describes how the Wall was constructed by an army of laborers divided into pairs of work teams,
with each pair of teams positioned half a kilometer apart from each

other and instructed to build their respective walls until they met up in the middle. After unifying their corresponding segments, the teams would be sent to a different location and told to begin the process anew. It is frequently assumed, the narrator notes, that all of these individual segments have since been joined together into a single continuous structure, though he concedes that no one knows for certain whether this is in fact the case, given that the Wall's unity is not something one person can verify, at least not with his own eyes and by his own standards.[16]

Kafka posits that the efficacy of the Wall, together with the political coherence of the empire it was designed to protect, is rooted in a tension between the immensity of the structure and the piecemeal process by which it was constructed. He notes that the significance of the Wall lies in its status not as a physical barricade against external invasion, but as a symbol of the structural conditions that help grant the Chinese empire its internal coherence in the first place. The empire, he argues, is so vast that the common people in the outer provinces often don't know who their emperor is or even which dynasty is in power, and consequently the emperor's authority has merely an intangible, symbolic status for them. Paradoxically, the political cohesion of the empire is predicated on the vast gulf separating the emperor from his subjects; it is this distance that both renders the emperor effectively "dead" to his subjects and creates an imaginary space within which his influence may continue to live and grow.

Kafka's narrator concludes that the Chinese are plagued by a certain "weakness of imagination or conviction"—a weakness that makes it difficult or impossible to conceive of the distant emperor as a flesh-and-blood entity. Yet it is this same difficulty in imagining the emperor as a mere mortal that constitutes "one of the most important means of unifying our people," the narrator observes. "Indeed, if one may be so forward as to employ such an expression, it is the very ground on which we live. To supply detailed reasons for a reproach here would not mean assaulting our conscience but, what is far worse, assaulting our legs. And for this reason I will for the moment go no further into the investigation of this question."[17] Kafka suggests that the Wall's ability to generate a sense of collective identity resides in its status as a symbol of the gaps with which the empire itself is riddled. The emperor is impossibly removed from the vast majority of his subjects, yet this yawning distance— far from being a liability—is instead the source of his own authority. It is in the gaps between the emperor and his subjects that we find the stuff of legend, including the symbolic authority upon which the emperor's larger-than-life persona is itself grounded.

Just as imperial authority is, according to Kafka, predicated on the vast gulf that separates the emperor from his subjects, the Wall is grounded on the physical and historical gaps out of which it is composed. The Wall's effectiveness as a symbol of national unity lies precisely—and paradoxically—in its own inherent *dis*unity, just as its ability to anchor a sense of national identity is made possible by its status as a conduit of rumors and misinformation. In fact, our own relationship to the Wall follows a similar logic: We are never able to perceive more than a fragment of the structure at any one time, and yet we are constantly tempted to treat those fragments as representative of a larger structure. Our understanding of the Wall, in other words, is the product of a synechdochic process of using a part of the structure to stand in for the whole, exactly because the whole is ultimately nothing more than a loose assemblage of fragmentary parts. It is the existence of these gaps that demands a process of narrative extrapolation out of which a vision of the unitary Wall is then constituted. All of the gaps out of which the Wall is constructed—the structural gaps that separate the different sections of the Wall, the temporal gaps that lie between the different periods of Wall building, and the conceptual gaps that perennially intervene

between the physical structure and the terms we use to refer to it—
are bridged by the "stories" that collectively (re)create the Wall as a
coherent unity.

A real-world illustration of the role of these interregnums in providing conceptual grounds for imagining a unitary identity can be
found in a curious series of events that took place at the turn of the
century. On June 25, 1899, several Denver newspapers reported
that China planned to raze the Wall and use the rubble to build a
highway from Beijing to Nanjing. The Denver story was credited to
a Chicago businessman who had traveled to China to place a bid on
the project:

> I lived in China for four years . . . and during that time was interested
> in building a great many miles of railroad. While in that country the
> subject frequently was discussed by those in power as to the advis-
> ability of tearing down at least a portion of the historic wall and us-
> ing the stone for the purpose of making a roadway to Nanjing. The
> idea was to pulverize the rock and use it in the roadways. While it is
> not an assured fact that we will secure the contract we are now
> figuring on I am inclined to the belief that it is a possibility. The com-
> pany I represent has a capital of $650,000 in cash, and I have been
> instructed to use every effort to secure an opportunity of doing the
> work.
>
> Some of the wealthiest and best known capitalists of Chicago are
> interested in this enterprise.[18]

As a news story, this allegation that China was accepting bids from
foreign businessmen to demolish its most recognizable landmark
seemed almost too good to be true. And, indeed, the story ultimately turned out to have been entirely spurious—the product of a
Saturday evening meeting among several Denver-based reporters
who, frustrated that they didn't have any leads for the next day's
paper, resolved to fabricate one out of thin air. Realizing that a for-

eign story would be harder to debunk than a domestic one, they decided to concoct something about China.

An account of the resulting hoax was written up in 1939 by Harry Lee Wilber, a Denver writer, who added a curious anecdote about the hoax's afterlife. Describing how a Methodist minister named Henry Warren had incorporated the story of the hoax into a sermon about the destructive power of rumor, Wilber quotes Warren as having proclaimed,

> You may not realize, friends . . . the power of the printed word. Bad news and false news pick up added fuel and eventually blaze devastatingly . . .
>
> . . .
>
> As an example of the havoc that can be wrought, take the "Boxer Rebellion." The spark that set off the tinder in that terrible war was struck in a town in Western Kansas or Nebraska . . . by three . . . reporters who concocted and printed a wild yarn, for what reason I have never been able to find out, that the huge sacred Chinese Wall was to be razed by American engineers, and the country thrown wide open to hated foreigners.
>
> . . .
>
> This pure canard reached China and the newspapers there published it with shouting headlines and editorial comment. Denials did no good. The Boxers, already incensed, believed the yarn and there was no stopping them. It was the last straw and hell broke loose to the horror of the world. All this from a sensational but untrue story.[19]

It turns out, furthermore, that this account of the role of the Great Wall hoax in precipitating the Boxer Rebellion was *itself* "sensational but untrue." While it is well known that the late-nineteenth-century Boxer Rebellion had a distinctly xenophobic component and was fanned by rumors about alleged atrocities committed by foreigners, there is no evidence whatsoever that the Denver story played any role (and certainly there were no "shouting headlines" about the alleged demolition of the Wall in any major Chinese newspapers). The irony, however, is that even as the original hoax was being exposed, it was being transformed into a metahoax that, in turn, contributed to the understanding of the Wall at that particular historical moment.

This image of an endless chain of hoaxes and metahoaxes captures a crucial dimension of the Wall. The Wall is, in effect, the sum total of the stories that have been told about it. These stories are often only tangentially grounded on the material structure, and are to a much greater extent the product (like Warren's metahoax) of earlier narratives. What we regard as the Wall may therefore be understood as a marbled layering of stories about stories, to the point that even our understanding of the physical entity itself is filtered through those same stories.

It is in the Wall's status as a product of narratives that we find the secret of its historical resilience and power. Although the strength of the structure might appear to lie in its singularity, in reality its survival is a result of its ability to mean radically different things in different contexts. Able to symbolize everything from the nation itself to its remote frontier, the Wall's significance and function are constantly evolving to meet the needs of each new era, and it is this plasticity that has helped it remain relevant even when the world around it is continually evolving.

A similar point could be made about China. In modern Chinese, for instance, the nation is typically called Zhongguo—with the character *zhong* meaning center or central, and *guo* meaning nation or kingdom. Although the binome *Zhongguo* currently functions as a de facto abbreviation for *Zhong*hua Renmin Gonghe*guo* (literally, Chinese People's Republic, but more conventionally translated as People's Republic of China), the term's origins can be traced back to Warring States–period works, such as the *Mencius* and the *Book of Rites,* and even earlier to texts such as the *Book of History.*

During this period, the term *zhongguo* was used in two distinct ways—either in the sense of "Central Kingdom," to refer to the political unity presumed to have existed during the early Zhou dynasty, or in the sense of "central kingdoms," to refer to the various rival states that occupied China's Central plains region during the pre-Qin period of disunity. *Zhongguo,* therefore, has been used as a singular proper name, a collective common noun, and even as a plural term for an assortment of individual entities. It is in this latent lexical ambiguity, furthermore, that the contemporary term articulates one of the key characteristics of the national entity it denotes—suggesting that the nation is a plurality masquerading as a singularity, a fundamentally heterogeneous construct striving to reimagine itself as a unitary entity. It becomes clear, therefore, that what we currently refer to as Zhongguo may be regarded as a unitary entity only if we simultaneously acknowledge its underlying heterogeneity.

The Western name for China has an equally complicated relationship with its presumptive referent. There is suggestive evidence that the origins of the word *China* can be traced back to the third-century BCE Qin (pronounced "ch'in") dynasty. As early as the first and second centuries CE, for instance, the apparent cognates *Thinai, Sinai,* and *Cina* appeared in Greek, Roman, and Hindi texts. In China, however, no version of this *qin* root was used to refer to the nation *in Chinese* until the late nineteenth century, when the Euro-Japanese cognate *Shina* was reintroduced from Japan into China (where it was pronounced "zhina" and subsequently fell into disfavor on account of its associations with Japanese imperial aggression). To the extent that *Shina* is transliterated from the Western word *China,* which itself may very well have been derived from the name of China's Qin dynasty, the term's "return" to China in the nineteenth century could be seen as a transliterated transliteration of a transliteration.

The transnational circulation and mediated return of the name of

China's first unified dynasty, furthermore, roughly parallels the conceptual trajectory of the Wall itself. As I will discuss in the following chapters, the Wall that is regarded as one of the Qin dynasty's marquee accomplishments underwent numerous material and symbolic incarnations in China before becoming the Ming dynasty brick and stone construction that we see today, after which the *symbol* of the Wall continued to evolve within Western discourse into its current status as a national icon. Following the fall of the Qing dynasty in the early twentieth century, the Western view of the Wall as a symbol of the nation began making a return to China, where it was seen as representing everything from the country's imperial legacy to its powers of ethnic assimilation, and was eventually reappropriated as a national icon and a paradigmatic tourist site.

In the following chapters, I approach the Wall not only as a physical construction but also as a fantasy, an abstract ideal, and a locus of collective nostalgia. I argue that the Wall's contemporary existence is grounded on its continual destruction, just as its status as a symbol of national unity is made possible by the inherent *disunity* of the physical and historical structure. The Wall is a fundamentally fractured construct, yet it is this disunity that provides the basis of the contemporary structure's own coherence. To return to Lindesay's claim that the "Great Wall's greatness lies in its totality," I argue that the Wall is indeed a totality, but specifically *a totality of gaps.* It is in these gaps where the Wall *isn't* that we may find the key to what the Wall actually *is,* and it is in the interstices between the Wall's materiality and its potentiality that we find projected the desires and ideals on which the Wall's strength and power are ultimately grounded.

CHAPTER 2

Aspirations of Immortality

From this day forward, the practice of assigning posthumous
names will be abolished. We shall be called the First Emperor,
with successive generations of rulers being numbered Second,
Third, and so forth for ten thousand generations, and in this way
the succession will be passed down interminably.

—The First Emperor, attributed by Sima Qian, *Records of the
Historian* (109–91 BCE)

To borrow from the cluster of metaphors proposed in the preceding
chapter, one potential origin of the series of "hoaxes" (Wilber),
"gaps" (Kafka), and "explosions" (Cai Guo-Qiang) that have
yielded the Wall as we now know it could be traced back to a decision made in 215 BCE. It was in that year that the first ruler of a unified China—known as Qin Shihuang, or literally "the first emperor
of the Qin dynasty"—ordered his general Meng Tian to take more
than a hundred thousand troops and drive the foreign tribes out of
the northern regions of his newly unified empire. To preserve the
territorial gains from the resulting expedition, the First Emperor
further instructed Meng Tian to construct a line of defensive fortifications along the northern frontier of his new empire, starting
from the Gulf of Bohai across from the Korean Peninsula and extending deep into the Gobi Desert in Central Asia. The resulting
structure is regarded as the first iteration of what has now become

43

the Wall, and symbolizes not only the Qin emperor's success in unifying the rival feuding states in the Central Plains but also his alleged tyranny in governing the resulting empire. The dynasty collapsed in 206 BCE, less than a decade after the emperor sent General
Meng Tian on his northern expedition, but the memory of the frontier fortifications he built would long outlive the emperor, the general, and the dynasty itself.

Despite the significance this Qin dynasty wall has subsequently
assumed in the popular imagination, the fact of the matter is, we
know surprisingly little about the structure itself. Although there is
considerable archaeological evidence of early border walls in what
is now northern China, none of these physical remains can be dated
conclusively to the narrow historical window between Meng Tian's
215 BCE expedition and the collapse of the dynasty nine years later.
Not only is there scant physical evidence of the original Qin dynasty construction, the textual record is also surprisingly modest.
The most immediate account of the Qin Wall can be found in Sima
Qian's *Records of the Historian,* which was not composed until
more than a century after the Qin dynasty's collapse. Even this seminal text, however, contains just a few short passages describing
Meng Tian's expedition, only one of which specifically characterizes the structure as an actual "long wall" *(chang cheng);* the text's
other substantive descriptions of Meng Tian's wall refer to it as a series of barricades and barriers, but do not use the term that has now
become virtually synonymous with the Qin dynasty construction.
Despite the relative spareness of these descriptions, Sima Qian's
text remains the most immediate source for our knowledge of the
Qin dynasty Wall, and it is one of the primary inspirations for
the vast body of history and legend that has developed around the
structure.

Like the Wall itself, the origins of the emperor who allegedly ordered its construction are shrouded in mystery and contradiction.
Sima Qian records that the future sovereign was born in 259 BCE, in

the first lunar month (pronounced "zhēng" in modern Chinese) and that his father accordingly assigned him the etymologically related and nearly homophonous name of Zheng (pronounced "zhèng" and literally meaning "governance")—this name being particularly apposite for someone who would help put in place the institutional foundations for the next two millennia of centralized dynastic rule. Despite his auspicious name, Zheng's path to power was not entirely straightforward. At the time of his birth, his father—Zichu, known to history as King Zhuangxiang—was being held hostage by the rival state of Zhao, as part of a common practice wherein states would exchange members of their respective nobility as an expression of good faith. Zheng was therefore initially given the clan name of Zhao, rather than Ying, the name associated with the royal house of Qin, and the one by which he would subsequently be known. Zheng's paternity is further complicated by Sima Qian's claim, in *Records of the Historian,* that his real father was actually the merchant Lü Buwei, who had granted Zichu one of his own concubines (Zheng's future mother) not long before Zheng's birth. Regardless of the questions surrounding his origins and ancestry, Zheng inherited the Qin throne in 246 BCE, at the age of thirteen, and went on to establish the region's first unified dynasty.

The state of Qin was founded in 897 BCE, when the Zhou ruler granted a local horse breeder an estate in what is now western Shaanxi Province, on the condition that he provide the court with horses. This minor estate subsequently become an autonomous state that relocated its capital several times before eventually settling on Xianyang—located near what is now Xi'an, the capital of Shaanxi Province. Although the Qin dynasty is best known for its unification of the Central Plains region under the First Emperor, its military expansion actually began decades earlier. In 286 BCE, the Qin had conquered the kingdom of Song (itself a remnant of the Shang, the dynasty the Zhou had conquered a millennium earlier), followed three decades later by what remained of the Zhou ruling house. It was under Zheng, however, that the Qin's path to regional domination began in earnest. After he officially came of age in 238 BCE, the king's first conquest, in 230, was the state of Han, just down the Yellow River from the Qin. Two years later he conquered his own birth state of Zhao, to the northeast of Qin, followed by the states of Wei, Chu, and Yan. Finally, in 221 BCE the Qin ruler defeated the last remaining independent state, the state of Qi next to the Gulf of Bohai, and was therefore able to declare himself the single sovereign power in the entire Central Plains region.

Having presided over the expansion of his kingdom into an empire, Zheng concluded that *wang*, or "king," no longer accurately reflected his political authority. Therefore, he took the terms for the legendary Three Sovereigns *(san huang)* and Five Emperors *(wu di)*, who were reputed to have ruled China before the founding of the legendary Xia dynasty, and combined them to yield the neologism *huangdi*—which could be translated literally as "august thearch," or simply "emperor." After proposing to abolish the traditional practice whereby rulers were assigned honorary titles by their successors, Zheng proceeded to specify that he wished to be known to posterity as *Qin shi huangdi* (First Emperor of the Qin), which is now typically shortened to Qin Shihuang. The emperor further decreed that his son would be known as the Second Emperor, his grandson as the Third Emperor, and so forth down to the "ten-thousandth generation." This act of self-identification, however, proved to be somewhat premature. While the Qin ruler did succeed in dictating how he and his son would be known to history, his dynasty collapsed after the death of his son, and his original vision of an interminable line of succession was cut short before fully reaching its third generation.

Even as the First Emperor was speculating grandiosely about his imperial line stretching far into the future, he was trying to assert a clear break with the past. Specifically, he attempted to leave his mark on history by extending his centralization efforts from a purely political level to an institutional one, calling for the standardization of the nation's script, its monetary system, its system of weights and measures, and even the width of carriage axles so that all carriage wheels would fit into a uniform set of ruts in the roads. To facilitate transportation and communication throughout the unified territory, the emperor called for the construction of the Direct Road (running northward from the capital, Xianyang, to the city of Jiuyuan, near the Qin border), together with the creation of a national postal system. The emperor's endeavors also extended to a number of less progressive measures, including the burning of all books, out of concern that they might be employed by those seeking to "use the past to criticize the present"—exempting only texts on practical subjects such as medicine, agriculture, and divination. When Confucian scholars protested this edict, the First Emperor allegedly responded by burying several hundred of them alive.

Despite the emperor's notorious reputation for book burning and scholar burying, most of what we know about him comes from an influential book by a pair of Confucian scholars: the second-century BCE *Records of the Historian,* begun under the supervision of Han court astrologer/scribe Sima Tan and completed by his son, Sima Qian. Composed between 109 and 91 BCE, this text presents a systematic historical overview from the legendary Yellow Emperor up through Sima Qian's own emperor, Emperor Han Wudi. *Records of the Historian* is regarded as the first of China's official dynastic histories, and its careful structure, attention to detail, and rhetorical skill have helped earn it a preeminent reputation within early Chinese historiography. The text brings together information from a variety of sources to present not only a narrative account of the Qin dynasty, but also a historical genealogy that peers back to the preceding Zhou dynasty and even earlier.

In addition to its general historical objectives, *Records of the Historian* may well have had a rather more personal edge. In 99 BCE, Sima Qian had gotten embroiled in a controversy involving a Han general who had led an attack against the northern Xiongnu tribes before eventually being defeated and captured. When Sima Qian expressed support for the general, Emperor Wu took it as a personal betrayal, and sentenced him to death. The sentence was eventually commuted to castration, and upon being released from prison Sima Qian declined to take his own life—as would have been customary for an official who had suffered such a disgrace—and instead resolved to devote the remainder of his life to completing the monumental historical project his father had begun before him.

Some modern historians have argued that the book-burning and scholar-burying sections of Sima Qian's text are so beyond the pale that they must have been introduced by a different hand after the text was already completed. This may well be true, but to the extent that we might doubt the veracity of these reports of the emperor's notorious brutality, we might also question some of the descriptions of his remarkable achievements. Could all of the standardization and construction projects attributed to him realistically have been completed under his reign, or might they have been proposed as mere goals or ideals? Did the First Emperor *really* oversee the complete standardization of the nation's writing system, its monetary system, and its postal system? Did he *really* oversee the construction of the Direct Road and a canal linking the Xiang and Li rivers? And what of the Wall, the emperor's most notorious accomplishment and one that has subsequently become one of the most resonant symbols of his tyranny?

Apart from a handful of passing references, Sima Qian's text contains only two detailed discussions of the structure—the first in the chapter on Meng Tian's biography (chapter 88), and the second in a chapter on the Xiongnu (chapter 110). Both passages present the same basic information regarding the Wall's trajectory and the historical circumstances of its creation, and neither provides much detail regarding the structure's composition or the process of its construction. I will begin by considering the passage from the Meng

Tian chapter, and will turn to the parallel Xiongnu discussion in Chapter 3.

Even after the Qin conquered its final rival (the state of Qi) in 221 BCE and established itself as the preeminent authority throughout the Central Plains region, the new dynasty continued to be plagued by attacks from the northern pastoral-nomadic tribes— variously identified in Han historical texts as the Xiongnu, the Hu, and the Rong and Di. In 215 BCE, an envoy the emperor had sent in search of elixirs for immortality returned and presented the emperor with a text containing the cryptic prophecy, "That which will destroy Qin is Hu."[1] The Qin sovereign interpreted this to mean that the northern Hu tribes (also known as the Xiongnu) were the primary threat to the Qin dynasty, and he sent his general Meng Tian to drive the Hu farther north and construct a line of fortifications to keep them there. As Sima Qian relates,

> After the Qin had unified all under heaven, Meng Tian was sent to command a host of three hundred thousand soldiers to drive out the Rong and Di peoples along the north. He took from them the territory to the south of the Yellow River and built a *long wall*, constructing fortifications that took advantage of passes in following the configurations of the terrain. These fortifications began in Lintao and extended to Liaodong, *stretching over a distance of more than ten thousand li*. After crossing the Yellow River, they wound northward, reaching Mount Yang.[2]

It is in this description of Meng Tian's construction of a "long wall . . . stretching over a distance of more than ten thousand li" that we find the locus classicus of the formal name used for the Wall in modern Chinese: *wanli chang cheng* ("ten-thousand-li-long long wall"). Beyond specifying the Wall's beginning and end points, however, Sima Qian actually offers surprisingly little detail here— or anywhere else in the text, for that matter—about the Wall itself. This relative dearth of detail concerning what is now regarded as

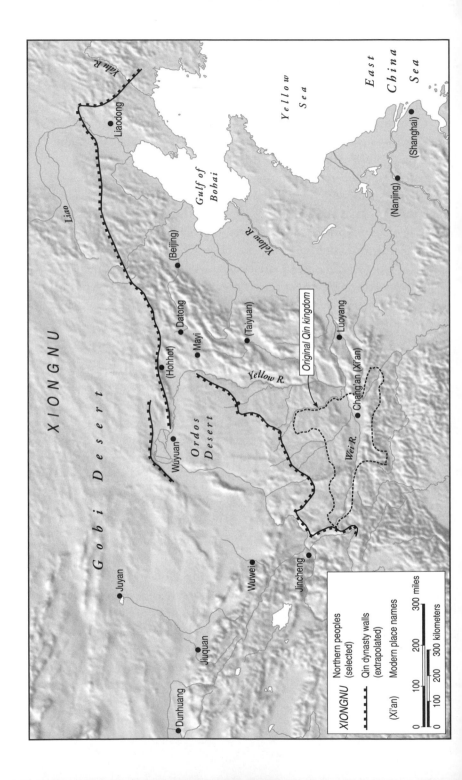

East China Sea

Yellow Sea

Gulf of Bohai

Yalu R.

Liaodong

Liao

(Beijing)

(Shanghai)

(Nanjing)

X I O N G N U

Datong

Mayi

(Taiyuan)

Yellow R.

Luoyang

Original Qin kingdom

(Hohhot)

Chang'an (Xi'an)

Yellow R.

Wei R.

Wuyuan

Ordos Desert

G o b i   D e s e r t

Juyan

Wuwei

Jincheng

Jiuquan

Dunhuang

XIONGNU   Northern peoples
(selected)

Qin dynasty walls
(extrapolated)

(Xi'an)   Modern place names

300 miles

100   200   300 kilometers

100   200   300 kilometers

0

one of the emperor's most ambitious projects has long perplexed Western readers. One modern historian, for instance, characterizes Sima Qian's description of the Wall as "casual and brief to an extreme," while another suggests that he "[treats] the building of the Great Wall like a summer picnic."[3]

Whatever the exact dimensions of the First Emperor's "long wall," it is clear they must have been comparatively modest. To begin with, Meng Tian had less than a decade to finish his work before both he and the First Emperor died and the Qin dynasty itself collapsed. Furthermore, even had Meng Tian been given unlimited time to complete his assignment, he still would not have constructed anything resembling the massive brick and stone structure we see today, given that at the time virtually all walls ranging from the walls of buildings to city walls to territorial "long walls"— were built using a more modest *terre pisé,* or "tamped earth," method of packing soil and gravel tightly between two wooden barriers and then incrementally raising the boards until the wall reached its desired height, with stone or rubble sometimes being used for the base.

The precise trajectory of the Qin dynasty Wall is not known. Sima Qian states that the First Emperor's line of fortifications extended from Liaodong, where the Liao River empties into the Gulf of Bohai in the east, to Lintao, in what is now Gansu Province, in northwestern China. From Sima Qian's specification of the emperor's desire to regain control over territory "south of the Yellow River," however, we may conclude that the geographic focus of Meng Tian's campaign must have been significantly more limited. Given that along most of its course the Yellow River runs well within the territory that was controlled by the nascent Qin empire, the only region where the emperor could have anticipated having *border* skirmishes south of the river would have been in the west, where the Yellow River loops northward through the Loess Plateau (which, incidentally, is also where it picks up the loess silt that gives the river its distinctive color) and then turns southward again before continuing its northeasterly route to the sea. Meng Tian's campaign, therefore, would have been primarily concerned with the area within this loop, known as the Ordos region—a combination of desert and arid grassland that was a natural fit for pastoral peoples like the Xiongnu, but which has presented a perennial defensive challenge for the Chinese societies of the Central Plains.

These questions of the Wall's physical composition and geographic trajectory bring us to Sima Qian's famous characterization of the structure as "stretching over a distance of more than ten thousand *li*." It is worth noting that Sima Qian uses the same word here, *wan* (ten thousand), to describe both the length of the First Emperor's Wall ("more than ten thousand *li*") and the length of the emperor's projected dynastic line ("and so on for ten thousand generations"). Just as the construction of a ten-thousand-*li*-long Wall illustrated the Qin ruler's vision of the virtual boundlessness of his new empire, his evocation of an imperial line extending for ten thousand generations expressed his desire for a virtually boundless dynastic reign. These assertions of the empire's territorial and temporal vastness, however, reveal an implicit anxiety about the dynasty's inherent limits. Despite Sima Qian's characterization of the Wall as a natural extension of the First Emperor's assertion of his boundless reign ("after the Qin had unified *all under heaven*"), for instance, he simultaneously notes that the emperor was motivated by a realization that his territorial authority was actually *all too bounded* ("Meng Tian was sent to . . . drive out the Rong and Di peoples along the north") and that his dynasty's grip on power would prove to be *all too finite* ("that which will destroy Qin is Hu"). It was in an attempt to assert the virtual boundlessness of his new empire, therefore, that the First Emperor created the Wall that would paradoxically become the preeminent symbol of the nation's boundaries and limits.

One of the most striking illustrations of the First Emperor's fascination with the possibility of unbounded power may be seen in the monumental mausoleum that was either being planned or actually under construction from the time he was crowned king of the Qin, at the age of thirteen, until his death thirty-five years later. An enormous structure that reportedly employed the labor of 700,000 men, the mausoleum remains unopened to this day, though Sima Qian provides an evocative description of its contents:

> When the Emperor first came to the throne he began digging and shaping Mount Li. Later, when he unified the empire, he had over seven hundred thousand men from all over the empire transported to the spot. They dug down to the third layer of underground springs, and poured in bronze to make the outer coffin. Palaces, scenic towers, and the hundred officials, as well as rare utensils and wonderful objects were brought in to fill the tomb. Craftsmen were ordered to set up crossbows and arrows, rigged so that they would immediately shoot down anyone attempting to break in. Mercury was used to fashion the hundred rivers, the Yellow River, the Yangtze, and the seas in such a way that they flowed. Above were set the heavenly bodies and, below, the earth's features. Oil from a sea mammal was used for lamps, which were calculated to burn almost interminably without going out.[4]

The Qin emperor affirmed his political authority by filling his final resting place with physical artifacts brought in from throughout his empire, together with abstract representations of the empire itself and of the cosmos within which it is located (though it is worth noting that Sima Qian does not use terms like *image* or *replica* in this passage, but rather describes the "heavenly bodies" and "earth's features" as if they were the real thing). In this way, the Qin dynasty is presented as a miniature version of the cosmological order within which it was located; by asserting a *representational* authority over the earth and heavens the emperor was implicitly reaffirming his own political sovereignty over the terrestrial empire he had founded.

One of the ironies behind the enormous mausoleum the First Emperor built for himself is that he appears to have had no intention of ever having to use it. Fascinated with the possibility of cheating death, he was determined to employ alchemical means to attain the same control over his own mortality that his armies had allowed him to achieve over his new territory. To this end, he experimented with a variety of pills and potions, and also sent several expeditions to the isles off the Bohai Gulf coast in search of elixirs of immortality. Although the First Emperor invested considerable energy in his pursuit of immortality, in the end it was this very quest that appears to have contributed to his death. Sima Qian recounts, for instance, how at one point some of the envoys the emperor had sent to the Isle of Penglai to retrieve elixirs of immortality returned empty-handed and reported that they had been stymied in their quest by several large fish. Soon afterward, the emperor had a dream in which he was battling a sea deity in human form—which was subsequently interpreted to mean that he must endeavor to drive away evil sea spirits and attract beneficial ones. The emperor therefore armed himself with a crossbow and traveled to the coastal mountain of Zhifu, where he found and impaled a fish, and it was soon after this that the emperor unexpectedly died. After the emperor's death, his chief chancellor, Li Si, directed that the death be kept a secret until the body could be returned to the capital, and when the odor of rotting imperial flesh became increasingly pronounced, he ordered that the carriages be loaded with dried fish to help mask the stench.

We might see the emperor's death, therefore, as the result of a sequence of events set in motion by his pursuit of immortality—a sort of karmic retribution, perhaps, for his killing of a fish that was itself a symbolic substitute for the one that had stymied his envoys' quest for elixirs of immortality. Furthermore, the fish symbolism in Sima

Qian's account of the First Emperor's death makes an uncanny return in his description of the lamp that would keep the emperor's tomb illuminated in virtual perpetuity. Sima Qian specifies that the lamp was to be fueled by oil from what he calls a *renyu* (a "man-fish")—apparently a reference to an aquatic mammal of some sort, but also implicitly alluding to the mutually intertwined fates of man and fish that lay behind the emperor's own mortality.

After the emperor's remains had been returned to the capital, the emperor's chief eunuch and chief chancellor destroyed a letter he had written to his eldest son, Fusu, instructing him to return and assume the throne. They then substituted an apocryphal letter ordering both Fusu and General Meng Tian to commit suicide, combined with a spurious imperial edict instructing that the throne be transferred to the First Emperor's youngest son, Huhai. Three years later, however, Huhai himself was forced to take his own life, thereby bringing to an end the empire his father had founded (while Huhai was succeeded briefly by the son of his half-brother, the Qin dynasty by that point had reverted to its former status as a kingdom, thereby relegating its final leader to the status of mere king, rather than emperor). In this way, the prophecy that "that which will destroy Qin is Hu" was ultimately borne out, although not in the way the emperor had anticipated. It was not the northern Hu tribes who brought down the nascent empire, but the emperor's own son, Huhai—meaning that the Qin's greatest threat ended up coming not from without, but from within.

Although the First Emperor died in 215 BCE and his dynasty collapsed shortly afterward, many of the political and social institutions he helped put in place long outlived him and the dynasty he founded. The Qin model of dividing the empire into separate administrative commanderies and counties, for instance, provided the basis for the province-county administrative system that has persisted up to the present, just as the court's efforts to standardize the transportation, communication, and monetary systems would be emulated, to varying degrees, by subsequent regimes right up to the current one. The immortality the First Emperor craved so ardently was therefore realized virtually, through the institutional models he helped conceive and implement.

A good illustration of the emperor's fascination with immortality can be found in the thousands of terra-cotta statues that were buried in three large pits about a kilometer from his imperial tomb. When these statues were discovered in 1974 by a Xi'an peasant digging a well, their existence came as a complete surprise, since the historical record makes no mention whatsoever of this vast army. Beyond the mere fact that they existed at all, these life-size figures were also astonishing for their sheer artistry and verisimilitude, which has no known precedent in Chinese culture. In fact, the statues are so realistic that it was initially believed that they were each modeled on actual individuals, though it turns out that they were created through a mass-production process using a set of standard molds, which were then individually modified to give the figures their distinctive facial expressions, hairstyles, and other details.

The discovery of the Qin emperor's funereal army happened to coincide with a general resurgence of interest in China in the Qin dynasty and the First Emperor. In 1958, for instance, Chairman Mao had famously praised the First Emperor in his remarks at the Second Plenum of the Eighth Central Committee, noting that "Qin Shihuang was an authority in emphasizing the present while slighting the past." He added, "Of course, I do not approve of citing Qin Shihuang either," to which his chosen successor at the time, Lin Biao, interpolated, "Qin Shihuang burned books and buried Confucian scholars alive." Mao then proceeded to riff enthusiastically on the topic:

> What did the First Emperor amount to? He only buried 460 scholars alive, while we have buried forty-six thousand. Haven't we killed counterrevolutionary intellectuals? In my debates with some mem-

bers of the minor democratic parties, I told them, "You revile us for being like the First Emperor, but that is wrong. We have actually surpassed the First Emperor a hundredfold. You revile us for being like the First Emperor, for being dictators. We don't dispute this. In fact, you haven't even gone far enough, and we need to supplement your criticisms!" [Laughs].[5]

While Lin Biao is not known to have made any further mention of the First Emperor, a document attributed to his son and released shortly after Lin Biao's suspicious death in a plane crash in 1971 accuses Mao of having "become a contemporary Qin Shihuang." The Chinese Communist Party (CCP) distributed this document widely to Communist cadres and the masses, exhorting them to "criticize this counterrevolutionary program of Lin Biao line by line and paragraph by paragraph."[6]

To the extent that alleged counterrevolutionaries like Lin Biao and his son were associated with criticisms of the First Emperor, it seems logical that the appropriate revolutionary stance would therefore be to support him. This circumstance contributed to the enormous popularity of a generally positive biography of the First Emperor published the following year by the historian Hong Shidi. Based on a longer and more scholarly 1956 biography of the emperor, the 1972 volume was an immediate best seller, and by the time the emperor's terra-cotta warriors were discovered in 1974 it had sold more than two million copies.

Not only did Mao praise his Qin dynasty predecessor, but his own reign suggestively mirrored that of his notorious predecessor. Both rulers presided over a transformative realignment of China's political system, and in each case their military, political, and institutional accomplishments were compromised by their reputations for ruthlessness and tyranny. Even the chronological trajectories of their respective careers mirrored each other with startling precision. Mao's tenure as the titular head of the People's Republic of China, for instance, is conventionally divided into the initial "seventeen years" from the founding of the PRC in 1949 until the beginning of the Cultural Revolution, and the decade-long Cultural Revolution that officially concluded with Mao's death in 1976. If we begin counting from when Zheng turned eighteen and began ruling under his own name, then his tenure as head of the Qin may similarly be divided into his initial twenty years as king of the state of Qin, and his final eleven-year reign as emperor of the newly founded Qin dynasty. Both rulers, in other words, spent approximately the first two decades of their reign establishing and consolidating their respective regimes, and the final decade pursuing an ambitious sociocultural revolution during which they formed a cult of personality as well as a reputation for tyrannical ruthlessness.

After Mao's death on September 9, 1976, his corpse was hurriedly embalmed (despite his express wish to be cremated) and later placed in a crystal coffin in an elaborate mausoleum built in Beijing's Tiananmen Square. This structure incorporated material from all corners of the nation, with 700,000 workers contributing mostly symbolic labor (in a nod to the number of workers said to have built the First Emperor's own mausoleum). In stark contrast to the hypervisibility of Mao's mausoleum in the center of Beijing—the site is one of the city's most popular tourist attractions, despite perennial rumors that the corpse on display might be merely a wax replica—the First Emperor's tomb in Shaanxi remains unopened to this day. Even with the contemporary surge in interest in the Qin emperor, Chinese archaeologists steadfastly refuse to touch this holy grail of archaeological sites—officially out of a concern with damaging its fragile contents, but possibly in response to a more general anxiety about disturbing the deceased emperor's remains.

One of the most notorious examples of this sort of prohibition against disturbing an imperial tomb can be found in the so-called curse of the pharaohs that was popularized after one of the members of a 1922 archaeological expedition to Egypt died from an infected mosquito bite a few months after the team's historic discovery of King Tut's tomb. This death was attributed in contemporary newspaper accounts to an inscription in the tomb that allegedly read: "Death shall come on swift wings to him who disturbs the peace of the king." This malediction, however, was revealed to have been a fabrication, invented by an overimaginative reporter trying to spice up his story. Apart from the unfortunate victim of the mosquito bite, most of the expedition's team members went on to enjoy long and healthy lives.

Meanwhile, the legend of the curse also went on to enjoy a long and healthy life. It would provide the inspiration for the 1932 Boris Karloff movie classic *The Mummy,* together with its endless sequels and spin-offs. In one of the most recent iterations of the motif, Rob Cohen's *The Mummy: Tomb of the Dragon Emperor,* the legendary Egyptian curse is united with China's own semilegendary First Emperor.[7] The third installment of a blockbuster action/horror franchise, *Tomb of the Dragon Emperor* is set in 1940s China and features Brendan Fraser as the mummy hunter Rick O'Connell. The film begins with O'Connell's son accidentally unearthing the First Emperor's tomb and in the process resurrecting the mummified (or, technically speaking, "terra-cottafied") Qin sovereign. A Chinese Nationalist organization seeking global domination then attempts to march the Qin emperor's terra-cotta soldiers past the Wall in order to grant them immortality, whereupon the group led by O'Connell and his son resurrects the Qin soldiers that the First Emperor had buried beneath the Wall, and recruits them to help defeat the emperor and his terra-cotta forces. The work's appropriation of the curse-of-the-pharaohs conceit, however, rests on a curious paradox, insofar as the curse's implicit critique of the (Western) desecration of ancient imperial tombs is directly contravened by the film's generally positive depiction of the O'Connells as heroes trying to save the world. Not only does *The Mummy: Tomb of the Dragon Emperor* stop short of criticizing the O'Connells for raid-

ing ancient Chinese treasures, but the work itself also implicitly rep-
licates their act of grave robbing in its own appropriation, for com-
mercial purposes, of the Chinese legends of the First Emperor and
his Wall.

The West, needless to say, does not have a monopoly on the strategic appropriation of symbols of ancient China, and numerous
contemporary Chinese directors have similarly attempted to resur-
rect the legend of the First Emperor—seduced by his larger-than-life
reputation even as they struggle with the conflicting political implications of his legacy. This contemporary fascination with the Qin
emperor and his Wall is particularly evident in the work of Zhang
Yimou. A native of Xi'an (having been born near the former Qin
capital of Xianyang), Zhang is possibly the most prominent Chinese director alive today, and his success in breaking into both
the global market and the international film festival circuit has
brought him acclaim and criticism back home. Like the First Emperor, Zhang Yimou tends to do things on a monumental scale, and
his series of reflections on the legacy of the Qin ruler and his legendary Wall are all virtually unprecedented in their size and ambition.

Zhang Yimou developed the theme of the First Emperor's monumental Wall in the record-breaking $100 million Opening Cere-
mony he directed for the similarly record-breaking $43 billion
Beijing Olympics in 2008. Performed for a global audience in the
newly constructed Bird's Nest Stadium, the ceremony featured
thousands of performers in exquisitely choreographed homages to
Chinese culture and civilization. The First Emperor's Wall was featured in a portion of the ceremony celebrating printing as one of
China's "four great inventions" (the other three being paper, gunpowder, and the compass), in which 897 performers appeared en-
sconced within oversize reproductions of ancient movable-type
printing blocks. The performers proceeded to raise and lower their
respective blocks in carefully calibrated patterns, presenting the audience with a series of rippling mosaics of culturally resonant im-

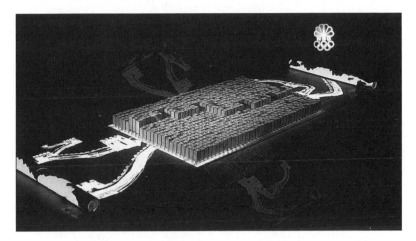

Image of the Wall formed out of oversize printing blocks, Beijing Olympic Games Opening Ceremony, directed by Zhang Yimou (2008).

ages. This performance culminated with the blocks coming together to form an undulating image of the Wall. The image was held for several seconds, and then the entire array appeared to burst into bloom as pieces of pink fabric emerged from the top of each block. Finally, the lids of the blocks flipped open and the performers popped their heads out, waving enthusiastically to the crowd.

This image of the Wall at the conclusion of the Opening Cere-mony's "movable-type" performance reflects the structure's status as an icon of both China and the Chinese tradition. The immediate dissolution of the image into a sea of flowers, meanwhile, could be seen as a commentary on the process by which the Wall itself is con-tinually being transformed and reinvented, while the subsequent emergence of the young men from inside the blocks evokes the memory of the laborers who are said to have been sacrificially bur-ied beneath the Wall as it was being constructed. In this context, the appearance of the performers also lends a human dimension to the uncannily precise performance, symbolically redeeming the actual labor that made the production possible in the first place. By using the flesh-and-blood performers who were literally positioned inside the contemporary reenactment of the Wall to allude to the legend of the laborers buried beneath the Wall itself, Zhang Yimou's performance critiques the Wall's traditional connotations of tyrannical exploitation while affirming the inherently performative dimension of the Wall itself.

Just as this segment of the Opening Ceremony celebrated China's invention of paper and printing, it also paid homage to the language with which those inventions were inextricably linked. Like the Wall, the Chinese writing system is often regarded as having helped unite the vast nation, even as it links modern China to the nation's historical origins. The Opening Ceremony's image of a Wall created out of printing blocks inscribed with Chinese characters, meanwhile, suggests a rather different perspective on the relationship between the Chinese language and the Wall—with Chinese functioning here as a symbol not so much of unity and continuity, as of fluidity and transformation. The Wall, in turn, is presented as a cultural construction mediated through—and embedded within—language, whose significance must therefore be "read" and interpreted.

Zhang Yimou's reflection on the Wall builds on a couple of earlier projects on which he collaborated with the Grammy- and Oscar-winning composer Tan Dun. In 2002, Tan Dun contributed the score for Zhang's first martial arts film, *Hero*—a work that, with an estimated budget of $30 million, was the most expensive Chinese movie ever made.[8] Four years later, Zhang returned the favor by directing *The First Emperor*, Tan Dun's debut at the Metropolitan Opera in New York—a project that, with an estimated $2 million in production costs alone, was the most expensive opera the Met had ever commissioned.[9] The Wall appears in both works as a symbol of the First Emperor's attempts to unify China, though they reach diametrically opposed conclusions regarding the significance of his legacy.

Hero is loosely based on the story of Jing Ke, an itinerant soldier who made an attempt on the Qin ruler's life when he was still trying to conquer the other Warring States kingdoms but was ultimately overpowered by the emperor himself. In Zhang Yimou's version of the story, the aspiring assassin—in the movie he is called Nameless—does not fail in his attempt on the ruler's life; rather, he decides at the last minute to spare his life, after concluding that the advantages to be derived from the emperor's unification of China far outweighed the violence and brutality that would be needed to achieve that end. Tan Dun's opera, meanwhile, takes its inspiration from the musician Gao Jianli—another historical figure who, like Jing Ke, is known primarily for his attempt to assassinate the future First Emperor. While the original Gao Jianli was actually a childhood friend of Jing Ke, Tan Dun reinvents him as an old friend of the Qin ruler. In the opera, the First Emperor attempts to convince the musician to compose the anthem for his nascent empire. Gao initially refuses (in protest against the emperor's brutality), and even after he accedes to the emperor's demands he undermines them by secretly basing the anthem on a song sung by slaves building the emperor's Wall. *Hero* and *The First Emperor,* therefore, mirror each other quite precisely, in that one work transforms an attempt to assassinate the ruler into an emphatic defense of the First Emperor's tyranny in the name of national unity, while the other embeds a critique of the emperor's legitimacy within an anthem that is ostensibly celebrating his authority.

Both of these contemporary works take as their starting point the emperor's obsession with immortality and our fascination with the assassination attempts that sought to bring a premature end to his grandiose ambitions—and both, accordingly, are concerned with how the emperor's vision of his own futurity intersects with our understanding of his historicity. These considerations of temporality and identity are developed even more suggestively in a film from near the beginning of Zhang Yimou's career. Although this earlier work, unlike *Hero* and *The First Emperor*, makes no mention of the Wall and alludes only tangentially to the First Emperor, it nevertheless presents an interesting perspective on the historical logic that helps shape our understanding of both the emperor and his Wall.

In 1990, four years after his directorial debut, Zhang starred in a Hong Kong flick called *Fight and Love with a Terracotta Warrior*.[10] Directed by the horror- and action-film specialist Ching Siu-tung, *Terracotta Warrior* opens with a love story between one of the First Emperor's generals (played by Zhang Yimou) and his beloved (played by Gong Li). Their romance is interrupted, however, when they are both sacrificed during the funerary rituals following the First Emperor's death. Zhang Yimou's warrior watches in horror as his love is burned in the imperial funeral pyre, whereupon he himself is caked with mud and buried alive with the emperor.

As it turns out, this double sacrifice on behalf of the Qin sovereign is only the beginning of the story. In an ironic inversion of the belief that the First Emperor may have been poisoned by one of his own mercury-laced immortality pills, Zhang Yimou's warrior is revealed to have inadvertently swallowed one of those same pills shortly before his scheduled sacrifice, and consequently he doesn't die after being buried but enters a state of suspended animation. He is reawakened more than two thousand years later when a biplane piloted by a young starlet acting in a 1930s spy thriller (also played by Gong Li) accidentally crashes through the earth covering the emperor's mausoleum. The warrior immediately recognizes the actress as his beloved but is devastated to discover that she has no recollection of her former identity. What ensues is a second romance, during which the reawakened general struggles to convince the starlet of her "true" identity until she is ultimately so impressed by his devotion that she decides to adopt the identity he has assigned her.

Fight and Love presents two distinct models for understanding the relationship between the past and the present. On the one hand, Zhang Yimou's warrior symbolizes what could be seen as a conventional model of history, in that he enjoys a continuous existence from the Qin dynasty up to the present. Gong Li's Shanghai starlet, on the other hand, represents a rather different historical model, in that she bears a suggestive resemblance to her putative Qin dynasty predecessor but nevertheless has no memory of that earlier incarnation. Imagined either as an amnesiac reincarnation or a coincidental doppelgänger, she symbolizes not historical continuity but historical rupture, and her connection to the past is extrapolative at best. As the relationship between the warrior and the starlet develops, she gradually begins to embrace her earlier identity for the sake of her suitor. By the end of the film, Gong Li's character has remembered—or constructed a memory of—her (putative) former incarnation, suggesting a model of historicity emphasizing the role of the present's *desire* to reconnect with its own past. While contemporary discussions of the Wall typically treat the structure as either a historically unified entity or a multitude of independent fragments, Ching Siu-tung's film concludes with a model of historicity that stresses the present's role in actively reaffirming its relationship with the past.

Just as Gong Li's starlet chooses to affirm her identification with the warrior's memory of his beloved, the relationship between the Wall and its historical antecedents can be seen as a product of retrospective identification. This relationship is real, in other words, precisely because it has been actively affirmed from the perspective of the present. Each new era doesn't directly inherit a preexisting Wall as much as it strategically appropriates an earlier body of beliefs about the structure to suit its own particular needs. Some of these beliefs may well be fictional or fallacious, but to the extent that they help generate future discourses about the Wall, they become part of the monument's actual history. Regardless of whether Sima Qian's description of Meng Tian's construction of the Qin dynasty Wall is strictly accurate or not, for instance, his *account* has played a critical role in shaping the ensuing history of the structure, as subsequent regimes have implicitly appealed to (or strategically rejected) the link between territorial border walls and imperial authority that Sima Qian articulated in his seminal text.

CHAPTER 3

Between History and Legend

There was a beginning. There was an anteriority before the beginning. There was an anteriority before the anteriority that was before the beginning.

—*Zhuangzi* (third–fourth century BCE)

At one point in *Records of the Historian,* Sima Qian recounts, in his typically dry and concise manner, an extraordinary tale of illicit romance, miscegenation, betrayal, and murder. He describes how, almost a century before the construction of the Qin dynasty Wall, the widowed mother of the Qin state's King Zhaoxiang (r. 307–252 BCE) had an affair with the "Rong king" of the Yiqu tribes to the north and bore him two sons. The relationship eventually soured, leading the queen dowager to murder her barbarian lover and send an army to attack his people and ravage his lands.

Sima Qian's discussion of the queen dowager's illicit affair and subsequent murderous vendetta is framed by discussions of two walls. First, this account of passion and betrayal is immediately preceded by a description of how—during the reign of King Zhaoxiang's predecessor, King Hui—the Yiqu had begun building "walls [*cheng*] and outer walls [*guo*] to protect themselves [from the Qin], but the state of Qin gradually ate into their territory and, under King Hui, finally seized twenty-five of their forts." The passage detailing the queen dowager's attacks on the Yiqu, meanwhile, is directly followed by a discussion of how the Qin state thereby came into possession of an even larger stretch of Yiqu territory, whereupon the Qin "built a long wall [*chang cheng*] to serve as a defense against the Hu."[1]

These border walls constructed by the Qin queen dowager and the Yiqu tribes constitute important antecedents of the Long Wall that the First Emperor is credited with having built in 215 BCE, though they also complicate our understanding of the Wall's significance. Sima Qian's remark that the queen dowager's construction was intended to offer a "defense against the Hu," for instance, is bitingly ironic, given that his own account makes it perfectly clear that the structure was *not* intended to protect Qin territory from external attack, but rather to help preserve the territory the Qin had obtained through its preemptive attacks on its neighbors. Indeed, the threat of Qin aggression is further underscored by Sima Qian's description of how the Yiqu were simultaneously building walls of their own to defend against the Qin. These descriptions of early border walls invite us to see the Wall as the product of a complicated symbiotic relationship between the Central States and their northern neighbors, rather than simply as a defense against those same neighbors.

Just as every wall literally has two sides, there are at least two sides to the story of the Wall itself, and embedded within Sima Qian's account of forbidden desire we find a startlingly unconventional view of the Wall's origins—a glimpse of the figurative back side of the Wall as we have come to understand it. While the preceding chapter outlines a standard view of the Wall as the product of the First Emperor's attempts to protect his nascent empire against attacks from the north, here we will take the border walls built by the Yiqu tribes and the state of Qin as our starting point for an alternative view of the gnarled and contradictory nature of the Wall's own historical origins.

Although the Wall is frequently imagined as an inviolate barrier built by China in defense against the pastoral-nomadic tribes from the northern steppe, the reality of the pre-Qin border walls points to a rather more complicated situation. Many of the pre-Qin "long walls," for instance, were built by Central Plains states to defend themselves not from northern tribes but from *each other*, while some of the northern tribes were building defensive walls of their own. Even the walls that were in fact built to defend against the northern tribes frequently developed out of an intimate relationship between the respective societies. King Wuling of Zhao, for instance, reportedly instructed his people to mimic the appearance and customs of the northern enemies, "to adopt Rong dress and to practice riding and shooting," and then used his enemies' own military tactics against them before proceeding to construct a "long wall" to defend his new territory. Around the same time, a general from the state of Yan was taken hostage by the Hu and subsequently managed to "win their deepest confidence," whereupon he used his knowledge of the enemy to defeat them and drive them more than a thousand *li* from the Yan border, and constructed a "long wall" to keep them there. In each case, the walls built to defend against the northern tribes were actually the product of a close interaction between the states in the Central Plains and the northern neighbors they were ostensibly trying to repel.

On the heels of his overview of the Qin, Zhao, and Yan border walls in the Xiongnu chapter of *Records of the Historian,* Sima Qian presents his second and final substantive discussion of the Qin dynasty Wall:

> The Qin finally overthrew the other six states, and the First Emperor of the Qin dispatched Meng Tian to lead a force of one hundred thousand men north to attack the Hu. He seized control of all the lands south of the Yellow River and established a border/barricade along the river, constructing forty-four walled towns overlooking the river and manning them with convict laborers transported to the

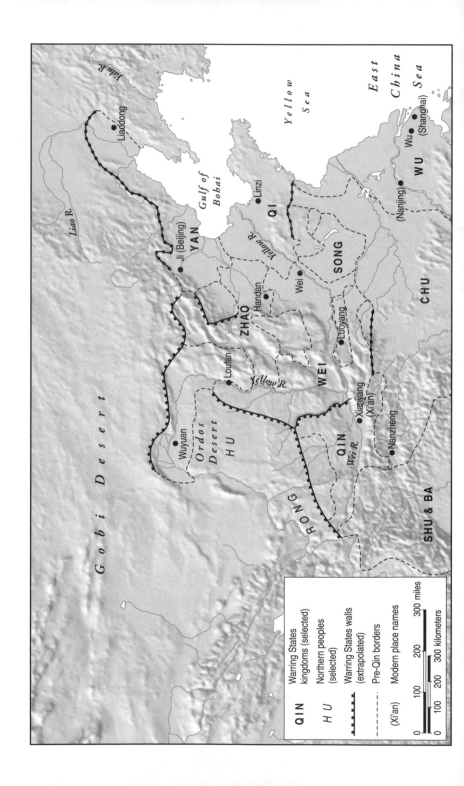

border for garrison duty. He also built the Direct Road from Jiuyuan to Yunyang. Then, he utilized the natural mountain barriers to establish border defenses, scooping out the valleys and constructing ramparts and building installations at other points where they were needed. The whole line of defenses stretched over ten thousand *li* from Lintao to Liaodong, and even extended across the Yellow River and through Yangshan and Beijia.[2]

Aside from a few minor changes (such as paring down the estimate of the number of troops under Meng Tian's command from 300,000 to 100,000), Sima Qian presents the same basic information here as in the earlier passage of *Records of the Historian* discussed in Chapter 2. To a modern reader, however, the most salient discrepancy between the two texts is that the passage in the Xiongnu chapter does not specifically call Meng Tian's defensive fortifications "long walls" *(chang cheng)*, but refers to them instead as *sai* (border/barricades) and forty-four *xian cheng* (walled towns). Sima Qian's failure, in this particular passage, to use the term that has subsequently become nearly synonymous with the Qin Wall is particularly striking given that he *does* use the term *chang cheng* in his preceding discussion of the border walls constructed by the kingdoms of Qin, Zhao, and Yan (which are frequently regarded as the actual antecedents of the Qin dynasty Wall).

This indeterminacy in the terms used to refer to the early walls is paralleled by that of the terms used for the pastoral-nomadic peoples against whom the Wall was ostensibly providing protection. While the Meng Tian passage refers to the Qin's enemies as Rong and Di, the Xiongnu passage calls them simply Hu. The names Rong, Di, and Hu sometimes functioned as ethnonyms for specific peoples on China's northern and western borders, but more commonly they were used simply to denote an abstract quality of "foreignness," or as stand-ins for the Xiongnu themselves. It is not certain how Sima Qian understood the terms in this particular description of the First Emperor's Long Wall, although the fact that he alternates among them in separate discussions of the same event suggests that he was primarily concerned with identifying the non-Chinese neighbors as foreigners or "barbarians," rather than with making specific claims about their ethnic identity.

Sima Qian's use of Rong and Di to identify the Qin's neighbors is further complicated by suggestions that the Qin itself shared, as one early text put it, "the same customs as the Rong and the Di: it has the heart of a tiger or a wolf, it is greedy and cruel and cannot be trusted when it comes to making a profit, it does not behave according to protocol, righteousness, or virtuous action."[3] This characterization of the Qin state as having the "heart of a tiger or a wolf" parallels Sima Qian's own description of the Qin emperor as having "a tiger or wolf's heart," and points more generally to a perception of the presence of an irreducibly foreign element at the very heart of what would come to be regarded as the core "Chinese" identity.[4] To the extent that early territorial walls were inspired by outside threats, these reflections on the interrelationship between the Qin and foreign tribes like the Rong and the Di suggest that the Wall was simultaneously helping to negotiate internal differences in the communities on either side.

To appreciate the ethnic tensions within the Central Plains states, it would be useful to consider a process of political unification that took place on the *other* side of the Wall, directly on the heels of the Qin dynasty's construction of the Wall. This unification was spearheaded by a Xiongnu by the name of Modun, whose historical significance could be compared with that of the Qin dynasty's First Emperor. As is true of the First Emperor, furthermore, most of what we know about Modun has been filtered through Sima Qian's *Records of the Historian* and its fascination with issues of paternal tension. When Modun was still a boy, for instance, his father handed him over to a rival tribe and then attacked them, hoping that they would then execute Modun in retribution. The son, however, managed to escape and return home, leading his father to decide to spare his life. Modun, however, never forgot his father's betrayal, and subsequently assembled a group of soldiers whom he trained to be absolutely loyal to him. To test the soldiers' obedience, he brought out his favorite horse and ordered the soldiers to shoot it with their arrows, summarily executing all of those who disobeyed. Next, he did the same with his favorite consort, again executing all the soldiers who failed to shoot her. Finally, when he brought out his own father, his followers did not hesitate when Modun commanded them to riddle him with arrows. With this act of virtual patricide, Modun not only repaid his father for the earlier attempt on his life but also managed to place himself in a position to become the supreme leader of the Xiongnu forces in the region.

When Modun seized power in 209 BCE, he managed to bring the various Xiongnu and other northern tribes together and establish a supertribal confederacy, of which he became the new leader, or *chanyu* (sometimes pronounced "shanyu"). We do not know much about the internal political dynamics that made this alliance possible, but it can hardly be coincidental that it took place just twelve years after the First Emperor founded the Qin dynasty, and just six years after the emperor sent Meng Tian to flush the Xiongnu out of the Ordos region. It seems likely, therefore, that it was the consolidation of the Qin dynasty, together with the dynasty's attempt to regain control over one of the prime grazing areas in the region, that provided the catalyst for the northern Xiongnu to form a unified confederacy. Regardless of the precise reasons for the Xiongnu unification, however, it is clear that the emergence of this new confederacy had profound implications for the states south of the Wall. Whereas during the Warring States period the Xiongnu and other northern tribes appear to have presented a comparatively minor hindrance to their Central Plains neighbors (who were generally more concerned with fighting each other), by the beginning of the Han dynasty the Xiongnu had developed into such a powerful force that the Han court was forced to recognize them as its equal, or even its superior.

The Han dynasty was established in 202 BCE, and its stability was immediately challenged not only by Modun's Xiongnu confederacy but also by several semi-independent potentates positioned along the dynasty's northern frontier. Tensions came to the fore in 200 BCE when the Xiongnu defeated one such potentate, who transferred his allegiance to the Xiongnu and even agreed to lead a rebellion against the Han emperor. In response, Emperor Gaozu decided to launch a preemptive attack against the Xiongnu and suppress the rebellion. The resulting campaign did not go well. Temperatures were frigid, and as many as a third of the emperor's troops are said to have lost fingers to frostbite. In the final skirmish, at Baideng Mountain outside the town of Pingcheng (near the city of Datong today, in Shanxi Province), the Han forces found themselves surrounded and cut off from their supplies by a significantly larger Xiongnu cavalry. After being trapped for seven days, the emperor finally managed to secure freedom for himself and his troops, but only after agreeing to grant Modun a sizable tribute that included one of the emperor's own daughters.

The Baideng defeat had an enormous impact on Han foreign policy, and contributed to the court's renewed interest in the political and symbolic significance of border walls. In a treaty signed in 199 BCE (and formally implemented the following year), the Han court negotiated a peace settlement with the Xiongnu, stipulating that it would regularly send the Xiongnu tributary gifts of silk, liquor, and wine, together with Han "princesses" to be betrothed to the Xiongnu leader. Known as *heqin*, or "peace-alliance marriages," this exchange of bribes and brides clearly constituted an admission of the Han's military weakness with respect to the Xiongnu. The Han, however, attempted to present the arrangement as being to its own advantage—on the argument that, as a result of marrying the Han princess, the Xiongnu leader, the *chanyu*, would thereby become the Han emperor's son-in-law, and the *chanyu*'s son would similarly become the Han emperor's grandson. By the codes of Confucian conduct (which Emperor Gaozu had only very recently embraced), sons of all flavors—including sons-in-law and grandsons—were expected to be filial to their elders, and the emperor's councilor recommended that court rhetoricians be sent to advise the Xiongnu on the importance of abiding by these Confucian precepts.

What we find here is a classic example of what Friedrich Nietzsche called *ressentiment*. Nietzsche developed the concept in his criticism of Christianity, which he said was a "slave morality" that attempted to transform a relationship of physical inferiority into an assertion of symbolic superiority (for example, in the act of "turning the other cheek"), and we find a similar logic at work in the Han court's attempt to transform its military inferiority with respect to the Xiongnu into an assertion of moral superiority. The Han claimed that its humiliating obligation to pay tribute to the Xiongnu actually placed the Han in a symbolically *superior* position.

The 198 BCE Baideng treaty marked a critical turning point in political relations between the Chinese and the Xiongnu, as well as a shift in the Wall's significance, from a symbol of martial aggression to an emblem of marital union. The *heqin* tributary system helped secure a relatively stable relationship between the Han and the Xiongnu, with the Wall coming to be perceived not as a physical barrier against external attack but as a symbolic boundary marking the outer limits of the Han's political authority. One of the most succinct articulations of this perception of the Wall as an abstract boundary between two civilizations can be found in a new *heqin* treaty signed in 162 BCE, which led the Han emperor, Wen, to declare that "to the north of the Long Wall will be the nation of those who draw the bow, which will be ruled by the Xiongnu *chanyu*. Inside the Wall will be the domain of those who wear hats and sashes, which will be governed by the emperor." To this, the *chanyu* replied, "The Xiongnu shall not enter through the Barricade [*sai*], and the Han shall not pass beyond it. Those who violate these instructions will be executed, and in this way both sides will be able to coexist harmoniously."[5]

As a result of the tributary relationship established in the Baideng treaty, the Han court was able to enjoy a stable and secure relationship with its powerful northern neighbors for the next sixty years, though at the expense of its ability to maintain a clear claim of symbolic superiority. During this period, the Wall continued to be imagined as an intransigent barrier between one region and another, even as its practical significance lay primarily in its position in a frontier zone across which people and commodities were exchanged and within which the relations between Chinese and Xiongnu were continually being negotiated and recalibrated.

Under Emperor Wu (literally, the "martial" emperor), who took the Han throne in 141 BCE, the fragile détente between the Han and the Xiongnu began to break down. The Han grew increasingly concerned by the Xiongnu's repeated violations of the *heqin* treaties already in place and the gradual expansion of their influence over the other pastoral tribes in the north. As a result, the Han court decided to resume a policy of military aggression against the Xiongnu, initially focusing on the same Ordos region that had been the object of Meng Tian's expedition nearly a century earlier. These military offensives were followed by a renewed interest in border walls, as the Han court began attempting to fortify its defenses along the northern frontier, and particularly near the Ordos region. Historians estimate that the Han may have constructed up to 10,000 kilometers of border walls, stretching all the way from Lop Nur, in what is today Xinjiang, to the Yalu River on the present border between China and North Korea. Remnants of this Han Wall are still visible today, including a relatively well-preserved section consisting of alternating layers of reeds and gravel near Yumenguan, in an arid desert region near the Gansu-Xinjiang border.

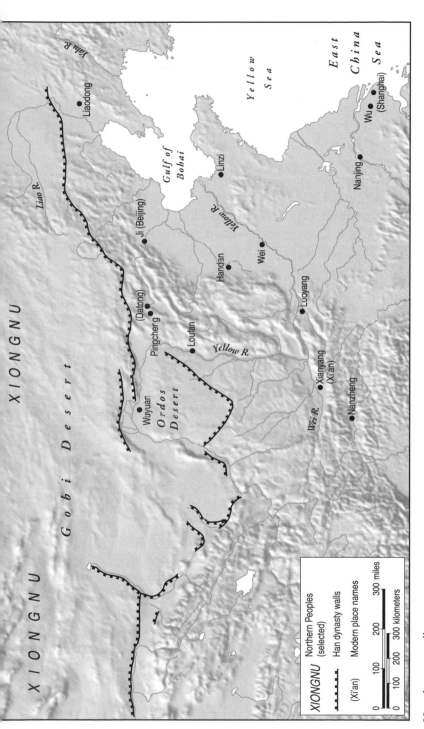

Han dynasty walls. Meridian Mapping.

Even following the breakdown of the post-Baideng détente, the Wall continued to be recognized by both Han and Xiongnu as a politically meaningful border. In the first-century CE historian Ban Gu's *Book of Han*—the dynastic history that picks up where Sima Qian's *Records of the Historian* leaves off—we find a Xiongnu leader in the first year BCE describing the Wall in neutral or even positive terms: "The territory to the south of the Long Wall belongs to the Son of Heaven [the Han emperor], while that to the north belongs to the [Xiongnu] *chanyu*. If this border Barricade is breached, it will immediately become known, and we will take no prisoners."[6] The Han Wall is presented here as not only keeping the Xiongnu out of Han territory but also keeping the Han out of the northern regions occupied by the Xiongnu, and in fact Ban Gu quotes the Xiongnu leader as having threatened to attack the Han if they attempted to venture out beyond *their own* Wall.

While the *chanyu* (in the discussion quoted by Ban Gu) uses the traditional term "the Long Wall" when speaking of the Wall as marking the limits of China's territory, when he turns to the structure's significance in marking the outer limits of the Xiongnu's own authority, he switches to speaking of it as a *sai*—borrowing a term that conventionally means "frontier" or "border," but which, in passages like Sima Qian's description of the Qin Wall at the beginning of this chapter and in the discussion of the 192 BCE *heqin* treaty cited above, appears to be used interchangeably to refer either to the border itself, or to the material barricades with which that same border is secured.

One of the best-known examples of the Wall's role in mediating between the Han and the Xiongnu can be found in the story of a Han woman whose name has become virtually synonymous with her act of *chusai* or, literally, "going beyond the Barricade." The woman in question was the Han imperial consort Wang Zhaojun, who is now celebrated as one of the four beauties of ancient China and who has been recently described as the "most heavily and continuously written about woman in Chinese history."[7] As the most famous beneficiary of China's *heqin* arrangement, Wang Zhaojun speaks to Han perceptions of the frontier territory separating them from—and uniting them with—their northern neighbors, as well as to the intersecting concerns with ethnicity and gender that have continued to inform the Chinese political imagination up to the present.

The first known reference to Wang Zhaojun appears in Ban Gu's *Book of Han,* where she is identified as Wang Qiang—with *Qiang* rendered with a character that means "wall." Wang's claim to fame results from her relationship with a Xiongnu by the name of Hu Hanye, who was appointed *chanyu* in 58 BCE and two years later managed, with the help of the Han emperor, to put down an attempted coup by his own brother. To express his gratitude for the emperor's support, Hu Hanye made three trips to the Han capital of Chang'an to pay tribute to the court, and on the third visit he asked the emperor to grant him a royal princess in marriage. The emperor responded by noting that while Hu Hanye's brother had committed several violations of ritual propriety (including, on one occasion, having had the bad form to execute a Han emissary), Hu Hanye, by contrast, had indicated he was willing to "protect the Barricade in perpetuity, as it stretches over hills and valleys all the way to Dunhuang in the West." He added, "Please call off the officials and soldiers stationed there, so that the emperor and his subjects may rest easy."[8] In the end, however, the emperor declined to grant him the princess he had requested, and instead offered him Wang Zhaojun, a lady-in-waiting who had been living in the imperial palace for several years awaiting the possibility that the emperor might select her to be an imperial consort.

After being married off to the Xiongnu *chanyu,* Wang Zhaojun went to live with her new husband "beyond the barricade," where she bore him a child or two (depending on the source). Following Hu Hanye's death, Wang requested the emperor's permission to "return to the Han" but was instructed to remain in the north. She did, and in accordance with Xiongnu custom, she then married her deceased husband's elder brother, with whom she proceeded to have one or two more children (again, depending on the source). Another Han dynasty text claims that after the death of her first husband, Wang was expected to marry her eldest son (or stepson), Shiwei, whereupon she reportedly asked him, "Are you a Han, or a Hu?" When Shiwei replied that he was "more Hu," Wang Zhaojun responded by committing suicide.

While these early sources differ on many of the specific details of Wang Zhaojun's fate, they all agree that she lived out the remainder of her days with the Xiongnu. Her traversal of the Han dynasty Wall, therefore, symbolized the role of the Han tributary system in securing a stable, long-term relationship between the societies on either side of this paradigmatic border, in a ritual of exchange that represents the Wall's own transformation from material barrier to abstract *symbol* of the border. Hu Hanye suggests that his receipt of Wang Zhaojun renders the actual defense of the Wall unnecessary, transforming it into a symbol of the peaceful coexistence of the Han and Xiongnu societies on opposite sides of the border it represents.

A rich and nuanced body of popular lore has developed out of this original kernel of Wang Zhaojun's story, with much of it focusing on the process by which she was selected to be the Xiongnu bride. While the original version of the story simply notes that Wang was chosen by the emperor, subsequent iterations offer a variety of perspectives on the process. The *Book of the Later Han,* for instance, specifies that Wang Zhaojun, frustrated by her inability to win the emperor's favor, had actually *volunteered* to be married to the Xiongnu leader. Another work describes how she declined to bribe the official court painter, who retaliated by rendering her very unattractive, with the result that when it came time to select five ladies-in-waiting to send to the Xiongnu leader, the emperor—who had never seen Wang Zhaojun in person—decided on the basis of her unflattering portrait that she was eminently expendable. In a roughly contemporary text, Wang Zhaojun is presented as a passive-aggressive figure who, out of resentment for the emperor's failure to notice her, refused to adorn herself and thus made him even more disinclined to notice her. When Hu Hanye visited the court, however, she dressed up in her finest clothes and makeup and volunteered to become his wife.

Wang Zhaojun remains an object of intense fascination today, having inspired countless essays, poems, plays, novels, paintings, and even musical compositions. She was featured in a 1923 play by Guo Moruo, a 1964 Shaw Brothers film, and a 1988 television miniseries. Her officially recognized tomb near Hohhot is now a major landmark, and there are more than a dozen other sites in the region that also claim to hold her remains. One reason for the perennial interest in her story is that her experience symbolizes the ethnic tensions that have long haunted the Chinese nation, and also represents the possibility of their eventual resolution. The literal exchange of her person between the Chinese and Xiongnu leaders, meanwhile, anticipates the virtual exchange and circulation of her *stories* through China and beyond—suggesting that these stories similarly represent China's ethnic tensions and a desire for their transcendence.

Another woman whose story has become inextricably intertwined with that of the Wall is Meng Jiangnü, or "Lady Meng Jiang"—whose tears are reputed to have brought about the collapse of the Wall itself. In the earliest iterations of this legend, the protagonist is not given a name of her own but is merely identified by her relationship to her husband, Qi Liang. Even after she began to be identified as Meng Jiang during the Tang dynasty, there remained disagreement over what precisely the name signified. Some versions of the story treated Meng as the woman's surname and Jiang as her given name, while others treated both Meng and Jiang as surnames (presenting her as the offspring of the Meng and Jiang families).

Some even used Mengjiang as her given name and assigned her a different surname altogether.

Unlike the story of Wang Zhaojun, the original source of which can be identified with a fair degree of precision, the historical origins of the Lady Meng Jiang legend are as murky as those of the Wall itself. We find a suggestive clue to the historical provenance of this legend buried behind a makeshift barricade in one of the famous Mogao Caves near the city of Dunhuang. Located in remote Gansu Province near an oasis along the trans-Asiatic trade route known as the Silk Road, these caves were used by Buddhist monks beginning around the fourth century to store scriptures and other texts. In the eleventh century, several of the inner caves were sealed off and their existence was largely forgotten, while the outer caves continued to be used until around the fourteenth century, whereupon they too were abandoned. When an itinerant Taoist monk by the name of Wang Yuanlu happened on the caves in the 1890s, he appointed himself their unofficial guardian and set about trying to restore and preserve what he could of their contents.

One day in 1900, Wang Yuanlu noticed a walled-off area in a corridor leading to one of the main caves, and upon knocking down this barrier he discovered a small room—now known as Cave 17 or the Library Cave—containing hundreds of thousands of ancient manuscripts. Thanks to having been sealed off for centuries, and owing to the arid climate of the region, many of the documents were in remarkably good condition. The collection comprised numerous Buddhist, Taoist, Nestorian, and Manichaean scriptures, together with other religious texts (including a copy of the *Diamond Sutra* from 868 that is the oldest dated printed text in the world). In addition, the cave contained a trove of social and literary documents, some of which were preserved only because they happened to be written on pages that had subsequently been recycled for copying Buddhist sutras on the reverse side. Coming just a year after a couple of epigraphers in Beijing noticed—on bone fragments used as a popular remedy for malaria—mysterious markings that subsequently proved to be the first traces of the 3,000-year-old Shang dynasty oracle bone inscriptions that would revolutionize historians' understanding of early China, Wang Yuanlu's discovery of the Dunhuang manuscripts similarly offered a remarkable and unexpected insight into medieval Chinese political, social, and intellectual culture.

It took Wang Yuanlu several years before he was able to interest others in his find, but eventually several international expeditions descended on the area, including teams led by the Anglo-Hungarian archaeologist Aurel Stein and the French Sinologist Paul Pelliot, who managed to convince Wang Yuanlu to sell them tens of thousands of scrolls and other documents from the caves. One of the Dunhuang documents that ended up in the Bibliothèque nationale in Paris was a short, anonymous verse that is the earliest known text to identify Lady Meng Jiang by that name. The document dates from the ninth or tenth century, and tells the story of Meng Jiang and her husband "Fan Liang," who was conscripted by the Qin emperor to help build the Wall:

> Lady Meng Jiang,
> The wife of Fan Liang.
> When he left for the northern mountains, he never returned.
> She had sewn him winter clothes but had no one to deliver them,
> So eventually she had no choice but to take them herself.
> The road to the Long Wall
> Is truly difficult.
> [two characters illegible] snow blows all around at the base of the mountain,
> Where they drink alcohol in order to avoid food poisoning.
> You, who were so healthy and strong, please come home soon![9]

This lyric contains many of the elements that have subsequently come to be associated with the story of Lady Meng Jiang, including her husband's having been conscripted to work on the Wall and her own decision to take him his winter clothes. This version of the text, however, is very fragmentary and contains several miswritten and illegible characters. The name used for Meng Jiang's husband, for instance, is not Qi, as he was previously known, but rather the visually similar character Fan (*fan* means criminal, and some later versions of the legend would retain this character for its semantic valence, rendering the husband's name as *fan Qi Liang,* or "the criminal Qi Liang"). It is precisely in its fragmentariness and imperfection, however, that this verse dramatizes the haphazard process by which the Meng Jiang legend gradually assumed its current form.

A more detailed version of the legend can be found in another, roughly contemporary, Dunhuang fragment. This latter text is a rendering of Lady Meng Jiang's story in alternating prose and verse sections and, like the verse cited above, this one also refers to Meng Jiang's bringing down the Wall with her tears and her subsequent use of her blood to identify her husband's bones. The fragment begins with a verse description of Qi Liang's ghost appearing to Meng Jiang in a dream and describing the circumstances of his death, to which she responds by weeping loudly and exclaiming,

"I did not know you had met a violent end at the Long Wall!
As you say that your bones have been buried inside the Wall,
I do not know what more I can say."

Meng Jiang threw herself to the ground and wept to High Heaven,
Lamenting at length that her husband had died much too early.
A woman's determination till death can move rivers and mountains:
Because of her piteous weeping, the Long Wall collapsed!

The text then goes on to describe, in prose, how Meng Jiang discovered a pile of bones beneath the Wall, but could not initially be certain which of them had belonged to her husband:

The bones were heaped in a pile, so how could she choose the right ones? She bit her finger till she drew blood and sprinkled it on the Long Wall to display her determination. . . . As the drop of blood dissolved, it immediately penetrated [the bone] completely. Of all the more than three hundred [of her husband's] bones and joints, not a single one was missing.[10]

The text describes how Meng Jiang collects her husband's bones in order to give them a proper burial, but then breaks off abruptly.

Meng Jiang's attempt to make sense of the pile of bones she finds under the Wall and separate out her husband's remains provides a compelling metaphor for our own relationship with her legend. From an inherently fragmentary and incomplete body of texts, in other words, we attempt to reconstruct a coherent narrative of the evolution of the story of Meng Jiang and its relationship to the Wall. To find the origins of the legend, however, it is necessary to peer deep into the past and consider a body of texts that antedate all of the subsequent legend's most distinctive elements (including descriptions of the Wall and Meng Jiang's wailing, and even the specification of her name itself), and that tell a story that bears only the most fleeting resemblance to that of Lady Meng Jiang as we know it today. These early texts provide the foundation for an increasingly elaborate mythos, the gradual development of which resembled a process of ad hoc wall building in its own right—with each new iteration of the story borrowing selected elements from earlier versions, while in the process revising, expanding, and transforming them into something new.

Although "Meng Jiang" is not identified by this name until around the Tang dynasty, there exists a much older tradition describing an unnamed woman's reaction to the death of her husband, a soldier named Qi Liang. The earliest known reference to this story of Qi Liang and his wife can be found in a Warring States–period historical text known as the *Zuozhuan*, from which

Sima Qian drew liberally in compiling his *Records of the Historian.* The passage in question describes a 550 BCE attack on the city of Ju by Duke Zhuang from the state of Qi, and specifically mentions a soldier named Qi Liang under the duke's command. After Qi Liang is killed in battle, the prince of Ju allows his corpse to be retrieved and returned home. Later, when Duke Zhuang encounters Qi Liang's wife on the outskirts of town, he attempts to offer his condolences. Rather than accept the duke's expression of sympathy, however, Qi Liang's wife chastises him for the inappropriateness of the location and circumstances: "If Qi Liang were guilty of an offence, then you needn't offer condolences. But if he is not chargeable with any offence, then there is the humble cottage of his father [where you can convey your respects properly], so I shouldn't accept your condolences here on the outskirts of town."[11] Although this account features some of the same concerns with spousal devotion that underlie the Lady Meng Jiang story as it has come down to us, this particular iteration makes no mention of Meng Jiang (at least by that name), the Wall (or any wall, for that matter), nor any of the other trademark elements of the resulting legend. Instead, the text simply notes that the encounter between Duke Zhuang and Qi Liang's wife took place "on the outskirts of town," without even identifying the town in question (the town of Ju? Qi Liang's hometown in Qi?).

We find another version of the legend a couple of centuries later in the pre-Confucian *Book of Rites,* though this time with the additional detail that Qi Liang's wife had "wailed bitterly" when she saw her husband's corpse. Inserted here almost as an afterthought, the description of the wife's wailing subsequently developed into one of the iconic elements of the story as a whole. Meanwhile, the Warring States–period Confucian classic, the book of *Mencius,* also alludes to how the wives of Qi Liang and a fellow soldier named Hua Zhou both "bewailed their husbands so skillfully that they managed to change the customs of the state." The text then uses this description to illustrate a broader point about the appropriate expression of ritual protocol—positing that internal virtue will necessarily manifest itself through ritual performance or, as the *Mencius* itself puts it, "That which is contained within, will necessarily manifest itself without."[12] In contrast to the *Zuozhuan*'s emphasis on the importance of adhering to existing conventions of ritual propriety, the *Mencius* passage focuses on the way in which the wailing becomes the basis for a *new* ritual protocol, to bring about a "change [in the] customs of the state."

Collectively, these pre-Qin texts include virtually all of the key elements of what will ultimately develop into the legend of Meng Jiang's tears toppling the Wall—except that there is still no reference to the Wall itself. While it is true that in a later Western Han text there is a description of how Qi Liang's wife "wailed in the direction of the wall [*cheng*], and her tears were enough to cause a remote portion of the wall to collapse," even here the "wall" in question appears to designate merely a city wall rather than a territorial border wall.[13]

The story of the Qin Wall does not begin to be grafted back onto the existing legend of Meng Jiang until around the Tang dynasty. One of the earliest known iterations of the legend to feature a reference to the Wall can be found in an otherwise unknown text cited in a fragmentary eighth-century Japanese manuscript. In this version of the story, the Lady Meng Jiang character (who here goes by the name Meng Zhongzi) is a young woman from the kingdom of Yan who is bathing outside one day when she happens to be glimpsed by a soldier named Qi Liang, who has escaped from one of the First Emperor's Wall-building brigades. Meng Zhongzi insists that, given that the soldier has now seen her nude, he must marry her immediately in order to preserve her honor. He agrees to do so, but after they wed he returns to the Wall, where he is summarily executed for having tried to escape. When Meng Jiang learns of his death, she travels to where he had been stationed and weeps so bitterly that her tears bring the structure tumbling down, revealing an enormous pile of human bones lying underneath. At a loss as to how to distinguish her husband's bones from the others, she bites her finger in frustration. When the blood from her finger drips onto one of the bones, it is immediately absorbed. Meng Jiang realizes that this bone must be one of her husband's, and she proceeds to use the same technique to identify the rest of his remains and provide them with a proper burial.

In addition to grafting the Lady Meng Jiang story onto the parallel tradition of the First Emperor's Wall, this Tang dynasty text also alludes to the popular belief that remains of the soldiers and conscripts who died working on the Wall are buried beneath it. We find a reference to this tradition in a folk song often attributed to the *Book of Han,* in which the legend is cited as a justification for valuing daughters over sons:

> If you have a son, don't lift him up,
> But if you have a daughter, nurse her to your chest.
> Don't look beneath the Long Wall,
> As it is supported by bones.[14]

Chinese culture has long maintained a distinct preference for sons over daughters. Even early Shang dynasty oracle bones, for instance, feature inscriptions addressing whether or not an impending birth will be "auspicious" or not (with an "auspicious" birth being, of course, that of a boy). The value placed on sons in Chinese society is informed by a corresponding emphasis on the importance of preserving one's family name. This Han dynasty folk song inverts the traditional Chinese preference for sons over daughters, implicitly undermining the dream of patrilineal perpetuity that helped inform the Qin emperor's original decision to ensure his dynasty's survival by building the Wall.

These considerations of kinship and sovereignty are complicated in some later versions of the legend, in which Qi Liang is presented as a relative of the First Emperor's general Meng Tian, and Lady Meng Jiang negotiates directly with the First Emperor to help secure her husband's proper burial. In one set of variations on this theme, Meng Jiang promises herself to the emperor, only to throw herself into the sea as soon as her husband has been properly buried. Just as Wang Zhaojun—in one popular version of that legend—voluntarily offered herself up to the Xiongnu leader, Lady Meng Jiang strategically offers herself to the First Emperor, but for the express purpose of reaffirming her devotion to her husband, Qi Liang.

Not only do the Wang Zhaojun and Lady Meng Jiang legends combine a focus on the Wall with an attention to the significance of marriage, they also share a more general interest in ritual performance. Ritual in China has long been closely associated with Confucianism, which itself has a rather complicated history. Chairman Mao, for instance, was notoriously critical of the "feudal" philosophy, and repeatedly attempted to abolish it entirely, while the First Emperor was so suspicious of the Confucians that he allegedly burned their books and buried their scholars alive. Confucianism did not fare much better under the Han, as the dynasty's founder—the former peasant subsequently known as Emperor Gaozu—at one point notoriously expressed his disdain by urinating into a Confucian scholar's cap. It was, however, under Emperor Gaozu that Confucianism was formally introduced to the Chinese court. Ironically, what interested the emperor actually had nothing to do with the Confucians' teachings on morality and ethics: it was the purely practical benefit of their expertise in ritual. As Sima Qian recounts in *Records of the Historian,* shortly after the peasant-turned-emperor set up his new court, he realized that many of his followers were undisciplined former soldiers, who were

> given to drinking and wrangling over their respective achievements, some shouting wildly in their drunkenness, others drawing their

swords and hacking at the pillars of the palace so that Emperor Gaozu worried about their behavior. [His adviser] Shusun Tong knew that the emperor was becoming increasingly disgusted by the situation, and so he spoke to him about it. "Confucian scholars," he said, "are not much use when one is marching to conquest, but they can be of help in keeping what has already been won. I beg to summon some of the scholars of Lu to join with my disciples in drawing up a ritual for the court."

"Can you make one that is not too difficult?" asked the emperor. . . . "You may try and see what you can do. But make it easy to learn! Keep in mind that it must be the sort of thing I can perform."[15]

Shusun Tong obliged and came up with a set of court rituals that were simple enough for even the emperor to learn, and in return he was appointed Master of Ritual and awarded 500 catties of gold. Having been chosen by the first Han emperor purely on account of the appeal and simplicity of its rituals, Confucianism was subsequently designated, during the reign of the dynasty's seventh emperor, as the official ideology of the court.

Generally speaking, ritual performance is concerned with the relationship between inner substance and outer appearance, and although Confucian ritual is ostensibly predicated on the assumption that inner virtue will naturally be manifested through external propriety, in reality it derives its power from a potential *divergence* of performance and belief. That is to say, although philosophical Confucianism is ostensibly concerned with people's inner thoughts and attitudes, its ritualistic performances focus more on establishing a uniformity of external practice. To the extent that Confucianism ultimately emphasizes correct practice rather than correct belief, it encourages the appearance of social homogeneity while permitting individuals and groups to maintain their respective beliefs. When the first Han emperor pragmatically called on Confucian scholars to develop a set of rituals for his new court, he inadvertently stumbled onto what would become one of Confucianism's best-kept se-crets—that its success as an ideology is grounded, in no small part, on the practical appeal of its rituals.

Like Confucian ritual, the Wall's power lies in its status as a figurative screen onto which a variety of different meanings and be-liefs may be projected. It is this quality of being a pure surface, fur-thermore, that provides the foundation for the Wall's conceptual unity and historical continuity. Like the workers who are reputed to have been buried beneath the Wall to help strengthen its base, the Wall's "true meaning" actually lies hidden beneath its surface, and it is this inaccessibility that provides the ground for the structure's own unity and coherence. We tend to assume, in other words, that others understand the Wall the same way we do, and it is this *as-sumption*—rather than a concrete continuity of identity—that helps explain the Wall's uncanny resilience as a symbolic entity.

The First Emperor imagined the Wall as a symbol, and a symp-tom, of his dream of a dynasty that would anchor a direct pat-rilineal chain for "ten thousand generations," but in the network of pre- and post-Qin walls discussed above we find, instead, a very dif-ferent vision of the Wall based on a pattern of ruptured patrilines and exogamous circulation. From the Qin queen dowager's danger-ous liaison with the barbarian Rong king to Wang Zhaojun's mar-riage to the Xiongnu *chanyu*, we repeatedly find walls being associ-ated with women circulating *between* patrilines, rather than with the strict preservation of those patrilines themselves. These pro-cesses of wall construction and the symbolic circulation on either side of the seminal Qin dynasty Wall illustrate the fluidity that has permitted the concept of the Wall to evolve and adapt right up to the present, long outliving the First Emperor's original construction and the specific significance with which he sought to invest it.

CHAPTER 4

A Garden of Forking Paths

In all fictional works, each time a man encounters different alternatives, he chooses one and rejects the others; but in the case of the almost-undecipherable Ts'ui Pên, he chooses—simultaneously—all of them. In this way, he *creates* different futures and different temporalities that also, in turn, bifurcate and multiply in their own right. It is in this that we find the explanation for the novel's contradictions.

—Jorge Luis Borges, "The Garden of Forking Paths" (1941)

At the center of King Hu's classic 1967 film, *Dragon Gate Inn*—one of the most influential Chinese *wuxia* (sword-fighting or knight-errant) films ever made—there is a wall.[1] Positioned in front of the remote inn of the film's title, this dilapidated structure provides a convenient backdrop for many of the work's sword-fighting sequences. The wall is nondescript, only a few meters long and easily overlooked in the action-packed film, though there is one slightly extraneous element that subtly tugs at our attention: a large white circle painted on the outward side of the wall (each of the outer walls of the inn is also marked by a similar circle). This circle is literally a cipher, a mysterious element that draws attention to itself despite the fact that the film offers no explanation of its meaning. Precisely because it remains unexplained, however, the mysterious circular mark invites us to try to make sense of it.

The circle on the wall in *Dragon Gate Inn,* directed by King Hu (Union Film Company, 1967).

We might, for instance, see this wall circle as a symbol of peripheries, and specifically the geographic periphery of the Chinese imperium. The Beijing-born King Hu filmed *Dragon Gate Inn* in Taiwan, to which he had just relocated from Hong Kong; while the work's opening sequence is set in Beijing, the rest takes place in an unspecified location along China's northern frontier. Alternatively, we could see the wall circle as a symbol of vacated political centers. King Hu made and released *Dragon Gate Inn* in 1967, as the destabilizing Cultural Revolution was at its peak on the mainland, and the film's story unfolds in the immediate aftermath of a critical crisis of imperial authority during the mid-Ming. More specifically, we could even see the circle as a sort of spectral anticipation of the Ming Wall, for the iconic brick and stone Wall would subsequently arise out of a partial collapse of imperial authority that could be traced back to the precise historical moment in which the film is set.

King Hu's film opens with a voice-over noting the year: "China's Ming dynasty, in the eighth year of the Jingtai reign, which is to say the year 1457 AD." Specifying the date in relation to the current imperial reign was conventional during the imperial period, though in this case the (technically correct) reference to the Jingtai reign is complicated by the fact that the events described in the prologue actually took place only *after* the Jingtai emperor had been deposed by the same half-brother—the former Zhengtong emperor—he himself had previously replaced. The origins of this imperial reversal can be traced back to a crisis seven years earlier, when the Zhengtong emperor was captured by Mongols and was replaced by his half-brother, who became the Jingtai emperor. This historical narrative is well known, and King Hu does not spell it out explicitly. Instead, he proceeds to introduce the emperor's chief eunuch and describes the eunuch's imminent execution of the minister of war, General Yu Qian, for his alleged betrayal of the Zhengtong emperor following his capture. The prologue then cuts away to the opening credits just as the executioner's sword is about to slice off Yu Qian's head, and the main body of the film follows two of the general's adult children as they are exiled to the northern frontier and pursued by secret guards whom the chief eunuch has sent on a mission to assassinate them, for fear they might return to avenge their father's death.

King Hu was a notorious history buff, and it would be easy to view his film's depiction of executions, attempted assassinations, and secret guards as an allegorical commentary—in the Chinese tradition of "using the past to critique the present"—on the Cultural Revolution that was under way in China when King Hu was making his film. Here, however, we will consider the film's treatment of history as a reflection not on the present but on the historical period in which the film is set—and specifically as a reflection on the relevance of that period for the subsequent construction of the Ming Wall.

The mid-fifteenth-century moment in which King Hu's film is set constitutes the virtual origins of the Wall-building project that would increasingly absorb the court's attention for the remainder of the dynasty. This project, furthermore, did not constitute a direct continuation of a tradition of border-wall construction dating back to the Han and Qin, but rather emerged out of what had become a complex web of endlessly bifurcating trajectories of Wall-building practices and the traditions they inspired.

With the exception of the short-lived Sui dynasty, none of China's unified regimes since the fall of the Han had evinced much interest in border walls. The Tang, for instance, the first dynasty to succeed in unifying China after the fall of the Han, had strong ethnic and cultural roots in the northern steppe, and rather than build defensive walls to protect itself from its northern neighbors it sought to expand its influence in Central Asia. The Tang's successors, the Song, meanwhile, are generally perceived as having been almost too weak to build and maintain defensive walls. The Song was militarily overmatched by the Khitan-ruled Liao dynasty to its north and was forced to sign a treaty positioning itself in a subservient tributary relationship with the Liao. Roughly a century later, the Song was partially defeated by another northern group, the Jurchens, who forced the Song to concede the entire region of northern China where the Wall had traditionally run. Finally, the Mongols, after they established the Yuan dynasty, already controlled the entire Central Asia region and therefore had little need for defensive walls to protect them from foreign invaders.

Several of the kingdoms and lesser dynasties during this period from the Han to the Ming, however, were in fact enthusiastic wall builders. Following the collapse of the Han dynasty in 220 CE, there was a roughly three-century-long period in which the region corresponding to modern China was controlled by a series of overlapping kingdoms and minor dynasties, many of which were ruled by partially Sinicized pastoral peoples from the northern and western border regions. A northern tribe called the Tuoba, for instance, established a kingdom known as the Northern Wei and proceeded to unify northern China. A Tuoba prince is recorded as having constructed a "long wall" in the early fifth century CE to protect the border from raids from the north, and about sixty years later a Chinese official in the Tuoba court recommended that the court build additional border walls on a massive scale, both for the practical purpose of defending against attacks from the north and also to position the dynasty within a tradition of Chinese border-wall construction dating back to the Qin and earlier.

Several of the other northern dynasties that followed the fall of the Northern Wei are also recorded as having built border walls through the region, including the Northern Wei's own immediate successors, the Eastern Wei, together with the Northern Qi and the Northern Zhou. Shortly after the Sui succeeded in briefly uniting China in the sixth century, it constructed approximately 350 kilometers of walls along its northern border. While each of these pre-Tang regimes had strong ties to the northern steppe, their construction of border walls functioned to separate them from those geographic and ethnic origins while symbolically allying them with a practice of governance associated with the Chinese dynasties of the Central Plains.

The last regimes to pursue these sorts of northern border fortifications prior to the Ming were the Liao and Jin dynasties, between the eleventh and thirteenth centuries. The Liao was founded by the northern tribe known as the Khitan, and its military superiority over the Song dynasty to the south allowed it to obligate the wealthy Song to make large tributary payments, which the Liao then invested in building border walls deep in Central Asia to defend not against the Song but against other tribes even farther north (remnants of these walls are still discernible in Outer Mongolia and eastern Russia, where they are sometimes referred to anachronistically as the Wall of Genghis Khan). After one of the Liao's vassal peoples, the Jurchens, succeeded in overthrowing the Liao and establishing a dynasty of their own, the Jin, they proceeded to build a network of border walls through the same general region to defend against the Mongol forces. Like the Northern Wei and their pre-

Tang successors, the Liao and Jin dynasties were both ruled by peoples from the northern steppe who were in the process of trying to reinvent themselves as orthodox Sinicized dynasties. While the Liao and Jin border walls were not explicitly called long walls and were positioned significantly farther north than the border walls built during other periods, these structures can nevertheless be seen as part of a broader long-wall tradition—reflecting a process wherein peoples from the periphery of the Chinese imperium used border walls to ally themselves symbolically with the Wall-building tradition associated with the Chinese interior.

In contrast to the familiar vision of the Wall as evidence of a direct historical lineage linking contemporary China to its Qin dynasty origins, what we find in the post-Han period is a complex network of parallel and overlapping wall-building traditions, interspersed with lengthy periods during which there was little or no border wall construction at all. If we look beyond these bifurcations and interregna, however, there is suggestive evidence for the continuity of the *notion* of a unified Wall. Not only did legends such as those of Lady Meng Jiang and Wang Zhaojun help keep the memory of a unitary Wall alive within the popular imagination, there was also a rich body of Tang dynasty poetry that prominently featured the Wall as a familiar topos. Known as "frontier" poetry, these verses often revolve around the nostalgia experienced by government officials assigned to remote outposts at the margins of the empire, and they evoke the Qin Wall as a rhetorical anchor for their remote setting—despite the fact that the actual Qin Wall was by that point a mere memory.

Perhaps the most compelling evidence for the persistence of an abstract notion of the Wall, even when the construction of actual border walls was falling out of favor or being relegated to the political margins of China "proper," can be found in cartography. An iconic representation of a unitary Wall appears unambiguously on several maps from the Southern Song period, including one called

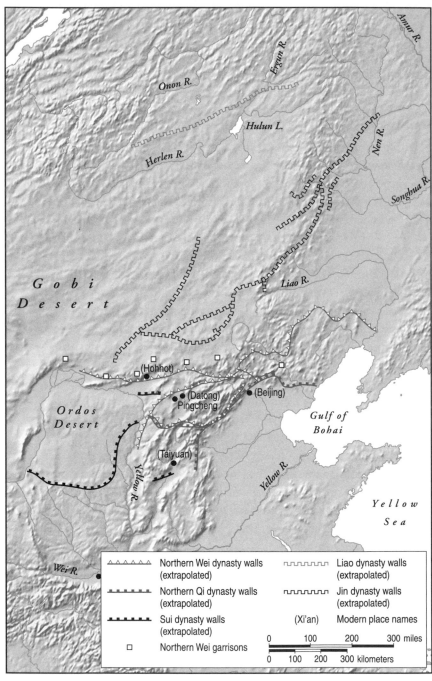

Northern Wei, Northern Qi, Sui, Liao, and Jin dynasty walls.
Meridian Mapping.

Map of Chinese and Barbarian Nations that was originally carved in stone in 1040, which presents the Wall as a continuous, crenellated structure extending from the Ordos region to the Gulf of Bohai. Similar representations appear on several other Song maps (including the *Geographic Map* discussed in Chapter 1), suggesting that the notion of a unitary Wall spanning China's entire northern frontier was still very much alive during this period, despite the fact that neither the Song nor the Tang had demonstrated any interest in border-wall construction, and the fact that the Southern Song no longer even controlled the territory through which the Wall ostensibly ran. While it is true that the Liao and Jin had built border walls of their own through the region, the general trajectory of the Wall as it appears on the Song maps corresponds more closely to that of the Qin/Han structure (as traditionally conceived) than that of the shorter and much more northerly Liao and Jin constructions. Accordingly, it would appear that what is being represented in the Song maps is not the actual Wall but instead a historical memory, and it was precisely through this cultural fantasy that the Wall persisted until construction resumed during the latter half of the Ming.

Although the Ming is known for its vast material investment in building its defensive Wall, the dynasty actually began with a very different strategic orientation. After rebel forces, led by a former peasant and temple boy by the name of Zhu Yuanzhang, overthrew the Mongols and founded the Ming in 1368, the court was initially not at all interested in building border walls. Instead, it attempted to follow in the tradition of the preceding Yuan dynasty and extend its influence over the various peoples living along its frontier. The Ming approached these groups through a combination of diplomacy and aggression, either granting them tributary status or attempting to defeat them militarily. The Ming court entered into nonaggression pacts with many of the surrounding polities while also establishing a series of border forts and garrisons along its northern border.

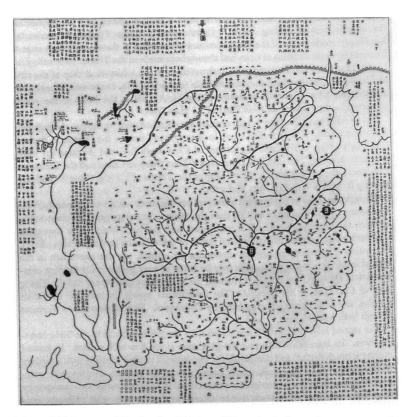

Map of Chinese and Barbarian Nations [Hua yi tu], Song dynasty map of China (1040/1137).

The Ming's expansionist aspirations were most evident under the dynasty's third ruler, the Yongle emperor. The fourth son of the dynasty's founder, Yongle came to power by seizing the throne from his own nephew, the Jianwen emperor, and proceeded to become one of the dynasty's most powerful and dynamic leaders. Between 1405 and 1421, for instance, he directed six of the court eunuch Zheng He's seven naval expeditions to destinations throughout

East Asia, the Indian Ocean, and even as far as the African coast. Yongle also transferred the dynasty's capital from Nanjing back north to Beijing, where it been located during the Yuan, and from this location he devoted considerable energy to extending the court's influence and authority into the region of the northern steppe. Between 1410 and 1424—coinciding closely with Zheng He's maritime expeditions—the emperor launched a series of military campaigns against the Mongols. These attacks did not fundamentally alter the balance of power between the Ming and the Mongols, however. After the emperor died during the fifth and final campaign, in 1424, Yongle was succeeded by a series of rulers who generally lacked his strength and ambition, and the court shifted from a strategy of military offensives to a reliance on tributary relationships with its neighbors.

The diplomatic crisis that provides the immediate historical backdrop for King Hu's *Dragon Gate Inn* was the product of a sequence of events that could be traced back to the appointment, in 1439, of a Mongol by the name of Esen Tayisi as leader of a tribal confederation known as the Oirats. Esen moved quickly to expand his influence within the region, and he also began dispatching increasingly elaborate tributary missions to Beijing, thereby requiring the Ming court to devote proportionally more resources to hosting the missions and reciprocating with "gifts" in return. The strain these tributary missions placed on the Ming court was exacerbated by a series of natural disasters in the 1440s, including multiple droughts, floods, famines, and bouts of pestilence and locust plagues, which affected virtually all regions of the country. The final straw came in 1448, when the Zhengtong emperor's tutor and chief eunuch, Wang Zhen, rejected an Oirat tribute, owing to what he felt to be the excessive compensation the Mongols were asking in return. During the ensuing negotiations a Chinese interpreter suggested that perhaps a solution could be reached that would involve having one of Esen's sons marry a Ming princess, but when Esen himself raised the possibility of this sort of *heqin*-style arrangement with the Ming court, he was unceremoniously rebuffed. He consequently resolved to launch an attack on Beijing the following year, and when the Ming learned of this threat it responded with a force of half a million troops, led by the twenty-two-year-old Zhengtong emperor himself.

The Zhengtong emperor's troops proceeded northwest from Beijing, through the Juyongguan Pass and past the Datong garrison, whereupon they encountered the remains of a Chinese advance guard that had been slaughtered by the Mongol forces just days earlier. Confronted with this corpse-strewn battlefield, the Ming commanders reevaluated their mission and concluded that it would be more prudent to return to the capital and simply *declare* victory. On their way back, however, the Ming forces set up camp at the Tumu postal relay station northwest of Juyongguan, where they were then routed by the Mongol forces and the emperor was taken prisoner.

The capture of the emperor had a devastating impact on the Ming court and immediately led to calls to abandon the Beijing capital altogether and relocate to the south. The emperor, meanwhile, was negotiating furiously in an attempt to secure his own release, to the point of agreeing—in what would have been an intriguing reversal of Han dynasty–style *heqin* arrangements—to marry Esen's sister and take her with him back to the capital. In Beijing, however, the court acted quickly to cut the Mongols' advantage by replacing the Zhengtong emperor, Zhu Qizhen, with his younger half brother, Zhu Qiyu. As a result, the newly promoted minister of war, General Yu Qian, was able to reject the Mongol attempts to ransom the captured emperor's life.

Realizing that his imperial hostage had become useless as a bargaining chip, Esen finally agreed to release the Ming leader the following year, in exchange for a token ransom. To secure his freedom, Zhu Qizhen agreed to formally renounce all claims to the throne, essentially bartering his imperial status for his personal freedom. Even his freedom, however, proved fleeting, as his younger brother, the acting emperor, imprisoned him as soon as he returned to the capital and kept him under house arrest in the Forbidden City for the next seven years. The political awkwardness of the resulting arrangement was highlighted by the Mongols' insistence on including, with each tribute they sent to the court during this period, a separate donation designated specifically for the former Zhengtong emperor—clearly intended to remind the Jingtai-led court of the unorthodox circumstances underlying its claim to power. After Zhu Qizhen managed to regain the throne in 1457, one of his first actions was to order the execution of General Yu Qian that is featured at the beginning of *Dragon Gate Inn*.

The Tumu incident, as the crisis came to be known, presented a fundamental challenge to the authority of both the emperor and the Oirat leader. Even after the Zhengtong emperor regained the throne, the underlying authority of the imperial institution continued to be seriously compromised by the political legerdemain that had allowed the court to preserve its power following the emperor's original capture. At the same time, however, things were going equally poorly for the Mongols. While in theory the capture of the Chinese emperor should have been a coup for Esen, it became instead a manifestation of his own political inefficacy. He had not been able to use his hostage to extract tangible concessions from the Ming court, and while he proceeded to declare himself khan in 1453, he was nevertheless assassinated following an internal revolt only two years later.

The imperial crisis, combined with poor economic conditions at the time, contributed to a pivotal reevaluation of the Ming's earlier expansionist policies. As early as the 1550s, following the Tumu defeat in 1449, the Ming court set about reconstructing and strengthening the walls and fortifications already in place in Juyongguan just outside Beijing, and over the next few decades it began to embrace the wall-building strategy that would increasingly dominate its attention and resources. Just as the Han dynasty Wall was built in response to the Xiongnu's virtual capture of Emperor Gaozu during the 200 BCE Baideng debacle, it was the Mongols' capture of the Zhengtong emperor at Tumu that provided the catalyst for constructing the Wall we see today. Both military setbacks underscored China's comparative military weakness vis-à-vis its northern neighbors, thereby encouraging the shift to an increasingly defensive and diplomatic strategy.

As had been true of Meng Tian's original Qin dynasty Wall, the strategic challenge that motivated the initial Ming dynasty Wall construction was centered along the southern edge of the Ordos region. By the mid-fifteenth century, the Oirat Mongols controlled much of the territory inside the northern loop of the Yellow River, and one of the Ming court's central concerns was how to contain the threat they posed to the Chinese communities to the south. Several proposals were made in the 1470s for launching expeditions to drive the Mongols back beyond the Yellow River loop, but they were all deemed prohibitively risky, and even had they been successful, the Ming court would not have been able to afford to provision the military bases that would have been necessary to control the region. During the Han and the early Ming, the court experimented with establishing permanent military compounds in the frontier region, with soldiers and their families farming the land themselves so that they would not need to rely on the court for provisions. In theory, the children of these frontier soldiers would inherit their fathers' positions, yielding a self-replicating population that would guard the border in perpetuity. The problem, however, was that these border regions were barely arable, and even efficient farmers (which the soldiers, presumably, were not) would have had considerable difficulty living off the land. Consequently, by the mid-Ming this model had been effectively abandoned.

Given that the Ming court deemed it militarily impractical to attempt to retake control of the Ordos, and politically undesirable to try to reopen formal trade relations with the Mongols, they therefore decided that one of their few remaining options was to construct a border wall along the southern edge of the Ordos region. The first such wall was proposed in 1471, when the newly appointed magistrate of Xi'an, Yu Zujun, petitioned the emperor to have a ten-meter-high wall constructed at the southern end of the Ordos to help defend the strategically important town of Yulin. This 1,700-*li* tamped-earth wall was completed in 1474, and was followed over the next couple of decades by a network of earthen walls throughout the southern edge of the Ordos (some of which are still visible in western China). In 1485, Yu Zujun recommended building a similar wall farther east, but this structure ended up being abandoned due to debates within the Ming court.

In addition to providing the foundation for the Ming's subsequent brick and stone Wall, these fortifications along the Ordos coincided with a broader set of diplomatic shifts that made subsequent wall building all but a foregone conclusion. In particular, the Ming court became increasingly disinclined to engage the Mongols through either diplomacy or trade, thereby—ironically—motivating the Mongols to acquire through military raids the goods and provisions they had previously obtained through tributary exchange. Those raids, in turn, drove the Ming court to build even more walls, making it even more disinclined to renew large-scale tributary relations with the Mongols.

In the mid-sixteenth century, the Ming began shifting from earthen walls to brick and stone constructions. These new walls were not only significantly more durable than the tamped-earth structures that had preceded them, but they also required a dramatically greater investment of resources. It has been calculated, for instance, that it would have taken approximately a hundred men to construct the same length of stone wall that a single man could build using the old tamped-earth method. These brick structures date to as early as the 1530s, and others were still being built when the dynasty collapsed a century later. While construction proceeded in a piecemeal fashion, generally speaking wall construction in western regions would push the threat of Mongol raids to areas farther east, creating the need to build additional walls.

The vast expense of these new walls had the effect of locking the Ming court into a defensive orientation wherein one of its only options was to continue building more walls. In the 1550s, the Ming court again debated whether to renew its attempts to drive the Mongols from the Ordos region but concluded that the cost of such an offensive would be unacceptable. The court instead focused its energies on continuing the wall building that was already under way, ultimately yielding the brick and stone Great Wall we see today.

Despite the Ming's vast investment in Wall construction, the Manchus continued their raids deep into central China up until the fall of the dynasty. The proximate cause of the dynasty's eventual collapse, furthermore, was not an invasion from without, but rather a rebellion from within. First, a peasant soldier by the name of Li Zicheng led an internal revolt and managed to take over Beijing. When he heard the news, a Chinese general by the name of Wu Sangui, who was guarding the Shanhai Pass, decided to allow the Manchu forces to pass through—apparently hoping that they would remove Li Zicheng from the throne. As it turns out, the Manchus did precisely that, but then they proceeded to establish *themselves* as China's new dynastic house. Thus, despite the vast resources the Ming had invested in building its Wall, its defenses were ultimately breached not on account of any material weakness of the structure, but as a result of the weakness of will of those assigned to guard it.

We may find a concise articulation of the logic underlying the construction of the Ming Wall in Walt Disney Studios' 1998 animated feature *Mulan,* which retells a famous legend about a young

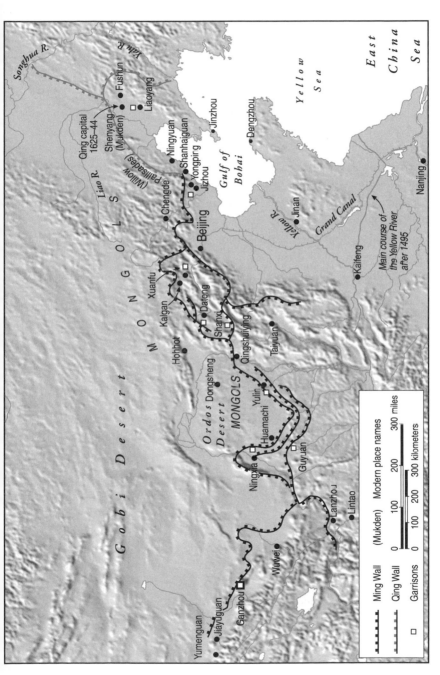

Ming and Qing Wall. Meridian Mapping.

girl who secretly dressed as a man in order to take her invalid father's place when he was conscripted to serve in the imperial army. At one point in the movie, the Xiongnu *chanyu*—or Shan-yu, as he is called in the film—states that by building the Wall, the Chinese emperor was merely challenging his (the *chanyu*'s) strength, thereby virtually *inviting* him to try to attack. Though set in a period approximately a millennium before the Ming built its Wall, this scene articulates quite succinctly the feedback loop that would eventually drive the Ming's Wall-building project, in that the construction of the Wall directly inspired even more of the same raids that it was ostensibly defending against in the first place.

While the Disney feature aptly summarizes the *logic* underlying the construction of the Ming Wall, the film's representation of the Wall itself is more problematic. The Hua Mulan legend is generally set in the period between the Han and the Tang, and this historical setting is corroborated by the film's specification that the northern forces are led by a Xiongnu "Shan-yu." The Wall that appears in the film, however, is essentially the brick and stone construction we see today and not the more modest tamped-earth structure that would have existed at the time.

This historical anachronism is not unique to Disney, and indeed an astonishing array of contemporary texts project a version of the Ming dynasty's brick and stone Wall back onto pre-Ming periods. For instance, when Eugene O'Neill (a well-known Sinophile who had repeatedly been tempted to write a play about China's First Emperor) wrote his 1926 play *Marco's Millions* a year after visiting China for the first time, he described the legendary thirteenth-century explorer Marco Polo encountering "the Great Wall of China with an enormous shut gate."[2] In John Ford's 1938 film on the same subject, the peripatetic Venetian, played by Gary Cooper, similarly enters the Central Kingdom through a gate in the Wall (with his father's burly accountant slung over his shoulders), and a more recent 1982 television miniseries directed by

Giuliano Montaldo—which happened to be the first Western production filmed on location in China since World War II—also has the explorer entering through a massive Wall.

The problem with each of these images of Polo's arrival in China, however, is that Polo himself made no mention of any such great stone Wall, or indeed any Wall at all. Commentators have long puzzled over Marco Polo's failure to mention the Wall in the travelogue he composed after returning to Italy, and some have even argued that this sort of omission is evidence that the Venetian must not have made it to China in the first place. I would suggest, however, that the more interesting question is not what this "omission" tells us about Marco Polo and his travels (or possible lack thereof), but what our fascination with the omission reveals about *our own* assumptions about the Wall.

Our knowledge of Marco Polo's journey is derived almost entirely from a text he dictated in a Genoa prison in the latter half of the thirteenth century. Replete with extraordinary descriptions of the life and customs of the Orient and of the magnificence of the Mongol court, this volume became one of the most popular and influential books of its time. Columbus, for instance, took a heavily annotated copy with him on his voyage to the New World, and Polo's description of Kublai Khan's opulent summer palace in Shangdu inspired Coleridge's famous description of the khan's "stately pleasure dome." Polo's travelogue helped plant the seed for a more general fascination with the Orient that would burgeon over the next few hundred years, and therefore it is fitting that his own entry into China is marked—in each of these modern adaptations—by his traversal of that most famous of Chinese icons, the Great Wall.

Marco Polo's family were merchants, and in the 1260s his father and uncle, Niccolò and Matteo Polo, made their way along the Silk Road across Central Asia to the Yuan capital of Cambaluc (Beijing). They were received by Kublai Khan himself and remained in China for three years until Kublai sent them back, along with his own ambassador and a letter to the pope. The pope, as it turned out, had passed away the preceding year, but as soon as a new pope was elected in 1271, he was given the letter the Polos had brought from Kublai and responded by sending them back to China bearing gifts for the Mongol leader. The Polos, this time accompanied by Niccolò's son Marco, again followed the Silk Road to China. They would remain there for the next seventeen years, during which time Kublai Khan allegedly appointed Marco to his Privy Council, and then made him a tax inspector in Yangzhou. In 1291, the Polos were permitted to return to Venice, where Marco regaled his friends and acquaintances with stories of his experiences in China. When, in 1298, he was imprisoned in Genoa during a military skirmish between Genoa and Venice, he dictated the account of his travels to his cellmate, Rusticiano de Pisa, and it was de Pisa who subsequently composed (in old French) the text we now know as *The Travels of Marco Polo*.

Although Marco Polo's volume came to be known in Italian as *Il Milione* ("The million [lies]")—so called by contemporary readers skeptical of its veracity—it nevertheless quickly became one of the best-selling and most influential books of the period. Initial doubts about the text's truthfulness, however, were reinforced as subsequent travelers bought back more detailed information about China, leading readers of Polo's volume to puzzle over its apparent omissions, including its lack of any reference to such distinctively Chinese elements as calligraphy, tea drinking, chopsticks, or foot binding. Some of these apparent oversights no doubt had plausible explanations. Given that Marco Polo was not well educated, for instance, it is not surprising that the Chinese writing system might not have made a big impression on him. It has also been observed that tea drinking, in Marco Polo's time, was popular in southern China but less so in the central and northern regions where he would have spent most of his time. Similarly, during the Yuan it was primarily elite women who bound their feet, and Marco Polo presumably would have had little opportunity to meet such women in person.

The omission that has caused the most consternation, however, was Polo's failure to make any reference to the one structure that had become virtually synonymous with the Chinese nation. As early as 1747, Thomas Astley asked skeptically: "Had our Venetian been really on the Spot . . . how is it possible he could have made not the least Mention of the Great Wall: the most remarkable Thing in all China or perhaps in the whole World?"[3] Half a century later, George Staunton, Lord Macartney's second in command during his historic trip to Beijing from 1792 to 1794, did some outside research of his own and came up with the following explanation:

> A copy of Marco Polo's route to China, taken from the Doge's Library at Venice, is sufficient to decide this question. By this route it appears that, in fact, that traveller did not pass through Tartary to Pekin, but that after having followed the usual track of the caravans, as far to the eastward from Europe as Samarcand and Cashgar, he bent his course to the south-east across the River Ganges to Bengal, and, keeping to the southward of the Thibet mountains, reached the Chinese province of Shensee, and through the adjoining province of Shansee to the capital, without interfering with the line of the Greater Wall.[4]

Staunton's meticulous account of Polo's route, however, is at odds with Polo's own account, which describes him traveling through the province of Tenduc, north of the Ordos. More recently, the British librarian Frances Wood has echoed and responded by making more explicit the suspicion that Astley had already articulated centuries earlier—namely, that Polo must not have gone to China at all, and instead was merely repeating and elaborating on stories he had heard from Arab merchants who had traveled to the region.[5]

Irrespective of whether or not Marco Polo ever reached China, there is a straightforward explanation for why his narrative makes no mention of the Wall: namely, that for all practical purposes there would have been no Wall for him to have seen. Polo made his journey more than two centuries before construction began on the Ming dynasty brick and stone structure we see today. The Yuan had displayed no interest in border wall construction, and even if Polo had encountered the remains of, say, the earlier Jin dynasty walls, those dilapidated packed-earth structures would not necessarily have captured his imagination. The recurrent astonishment at the absence of any reference to the Wall in Polo's travelogue, therefore, speaks not so much to the question of the authenticity of Polo's text as to the powerful anachronistic pull of our contemporary notion of the Wall.

Around the time Marco Polo's travelogue was published, a stream of Westerners began traveling to China as the Silk Road became an increasingly important conduit of overland trade between Europe and Asia. It was not until around the sixteenth century, however, that Western visitors begin alluding to the Wall, and even the initial accounts tended to be comparatively restrained. In 1559, for instance, Gaspar da Cruz noted that "the Chinas have an hundred leagues (others saying there are more) of a Wall betweene them and the other," while the legendary Jesuit Matteo Ricci, who was in China from 1583 until his death in 1610, notes that "to the north the country is defended . . . by precipitous hills, which are joined into an unbroken line of defense with a tremendous wall four hundred miles long."[6]

Even as Ricci and the other earlier Jesuits were describing a Wall of comparatively modest dimensions (at least as compared with the ultimate length of the Ming structure by the time the dynasty collapsed about half a century later), we find a much more impressive version of the Wall in a Jesuit map from the same period. Dated circa 1590, the map is considered the first modern European map of China and features an iconic representation of the Wall stretching

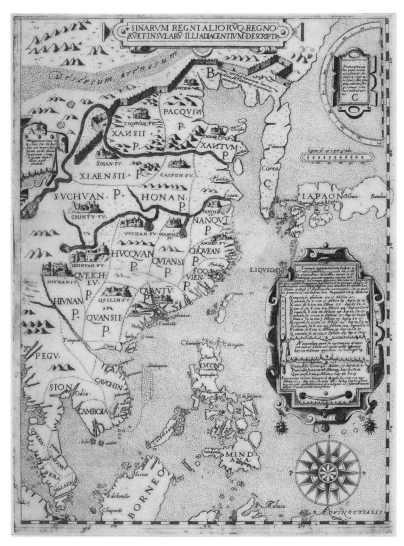

Sinarum Regni alioru[m]q[ue] regnoru[m] et insularu[m] illi adiacentium descriptio, anonymous, possibly after Matteo Ricci and Michele Ruggieri (ca. 1590).

Courtesy of the Hong Kong University of Science and Technology.

continuously from the Korean Peninsula straight across northern China to Shaanxi Province in the west. The map, titled *Sinarum Regni alioru[m]q[ue] regnoru[m] et insularu[m] illi adiacentium descriptio,* is unsigned, but the prominent designation of Ricci and Ruggieri's Jesuit church in Canton, labeled on the map "ecclesia patrum societatis" (the Church of the Fathers of the Society [of Jesus]), suggests that it was probably based on Ricci's own surveys and notes.

The paradox that this Jesuit map presents the Wall as being much more extensive than it appears in the descriptions by Ricci and the other Jesuits from the same period, may be explained by the fact that this Jesuit map was also drawn from indigenous Chinese sources. The descriptive table on the right side of the map, for instance, lists the administrative and regional divisions for each province and appears to have been borrowed from the sixth (1579) edition of Luo Hongxian's influential atlas of China, *Enlargement of the Terrestrial Map,* which also includes a distinct icon of the Wall (though earlier editions actually did not). Structured on a grid and visually rather different from the *Sinarum Regni,* Luo's map presents roughly the same configuration of China, including the same curiously narrow strip of Gobi Desert in the upper left (rendered in black in Luo's map). Most tellingly, both works present a similar representation of the Wall.

One collection of influential European maps that may have been partially derived from the cartographic tradition inspired by the *Enlargement of the Terrestrial Map* was the *Atlas Sinensis* created by Joan Blaeu in 1655, which was based on the maps provided by Jesuit cartographer Martino Martini. This atlas, the first European atlas of China, contains maps of each of China's provinces—several of which clearly feature an icon of a crenellated Wall—together with a map of the country as a whole, which similarly features a Wall stretching from the Gulf of Bohai to the Ordos. Martini himself noted that

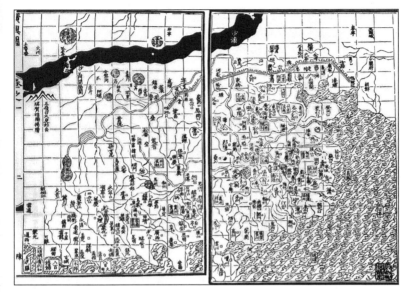

Enlargement of the Terrestrial Map [Guang yu tu], Luo Hongxian (1579).
Reprinted with the permission of Cambridge University Press.

this celebrated wall is very famous . . . longer than the entire length of Asia. . . . The person who began this work was the emperor Xius. . . . He built this wall starting in the twenty second year of his reign, which was 215 years before Christ. In the space of five years, which is incredibly short, it was built so strongly that if anyone was able to slip a nail between the cut stones, the builder of that part would be put to death. . . . The work is magnificent, huge, and admirable, and has lasted right up to the present time without any injury or destruction.[7]

Martini was, of course, mistaken when he claimed that the Wall constructed by the First Emperor had "lasted right up to the present time without injury or destruction," though his underlying *vision* of a "magnificent, huge, and admirable" Wall remains alive and well

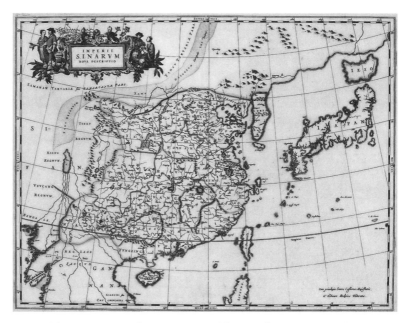

Imperii Sinarum Nova descriptio, Joan Blaeu and Martino Martini
(1655).
Courtesy of the Hong Kong University of Science and Technology.

even today. Transcending any specific physical incarnation or abstract understanding of the structure, it is precisely this vision of the Wall as an enduring monument that anchors its historical continuity and resilience.

By the time Lord Macartney led his historic mission to China in 1792, the Wall had already become a potent image in the European imagination. After the Macartney expedition visited the Gubeikou section of the Wall northeast of Beijing, several members wrote detailed accounts of the structure. Macartney, for instance, recorded in his diary:

> The wall is built of bluish coloured brick, not burnt but dried in the
> sun, and raised upon a stone foundation, and as measured from the

ground on the side next to the Tartary, it is twenty-six feet high in the perpendicular. The stone foundation is formed of two courses of granite equal to twenty-four inches or two feet. From then to the parapet including the cordon which is six inches are nineteen feet four inches, the parapet is four feet eight inches. From the stone foundation to the cordon are fifty-eight rows of bricks and above the cordon are fourteen rows; and each row, allowing for the interstices of the mortar and the insertion of the cordon may be calculated at the rate of four inches per brick.[8]

The extraordinary precision of these measurements reflects Macartney's intellectual and diplomatic training but may also have stemmed from a desire to assert a sort of intellectual mastery over this daunting structure. To the extent that the significance of the Wall traditionally lay not only in its status as a *physical* barrier but also in its assertion of *symbolic* mastery over the territory in question, Macartney's emphasis on the hyperprecise measurements of the structure could be seen as mirroring the symbolic function of the Wall.

The Macartney expedition's descriptions of their trip to Gubeikou addressed not only the Wall itself but also the reactions of their Chinese hosts. Macartney and Staunton note, for instance, that while they were investigating the Wall, their escorts merely gazed at it "with perfect indifference; and few of the mandarins who accompanied the Embassy seemed to pay the least attention to it."[9] While the "perfect indifference" that Macartney and Staunton attribute to their Chinese escorts is, of course, contrasted with the amazement that they themselves felt upon viewing the structure for the first time, it may well have reflected their hosts' ambivalent attitude toward the Wall that the Ming had tried to use to defend against the same Manchus who now ruled China.

A rather different perspective on the Wall's political connotations during this period, however, may be found in Staunton's description of an interaction the expedition witnessed: when "a Tartar, one of the attendants, [was] ordered to be punished by some of the Chinese mandarines, for misbehaviour, the man made a vigorous resistance, and exclaimed in a loud voice, that no Chinese had a right to inflect punishment on a Tartar after having passed the great wall."[10] If accurate, this anecdote underscores the Wall's contemporary status as the product of a double political reversal. First, the original strategic function of the Ming Wall was obviated after the Manchus overthrew the Ming and established the Qing. Second, the Manchus themselves immediately almost began constructing an extension of the Wall that commenced at the traditional eastern terminus at Shanhaiguan and extended east along the borders of the traditional Manchu homeland of Manchuria. Consisting of parallel earthen levees separated by a trench and planted with densely arranged willow trees—and overlapping in some sections with existing eastern sections of the Ming Wall—these Qing fortifications were designed to restrict Han (and Mongol) entry into Manchuria. In the Macartney anecdote, therefore, we find a Manchu servant remonstrating his Han superiors (who were themselves working under the ethnically Manchu Qing court) about respecting the sanctity of a border barrier that had originally been intended to keep the Manchus themselves out of China, but that had subsequently been partially reinvented by the Manchus as a barrier to keep the Han Chinese out of Manchuria—though it should be noted that the Gubeikou section of the Wall where the Macartney expedition witnessed this incident was actually significantly to the west of the Manchurian defense line.

Western and Chinese discourses on the Wall continued to diverge through the nineteenth century, with the West increasingly perceiving the monument as a transcendental symbol of the strength and resilience of the Chinese civilization, while in China the structure carried more ambivalent associations of the Ming's failed defense against the Manchus together with the First Emperor's notorious tyranny. A reflection on the Wall's bifurcated trajectory in China and the West can be found in a curious speculation in one of Henry Yule's notes to his extensively annotated 1870 translation of Marco Polo's thirteenth-century travelogue. Commenting on a passage describing Polo's arrival in the province of Tenduc, just north of the Ordos region, Yule observes that "it has often been cast in Marco's teeth that he makes no mention of the Great Wall of China, and that is true; whilst the apologies made for the omission have always seemed to me unsatisfactory." Yule then proposes what might appear to be a rather bizarre explanation of his own for this omission, noting that Polo makes a curiously mediated reference to the history of the "Tartars" by referring to what he calls "the country of Gog and Magog." Yule notes that Polo says, "Here also is what *we* call the country of Gog and Magog; *they*, however, call it UNG and MUNGUL, after the names of two races of people that existed in that Province before the migration of the Tartars. *Ung* was the title of the people of the country, and *Mungul* a name sometimes applied to the Tartars."[11] Polo suggests that the biblical terms *Gog* and *Magog* refer to two "races of people" that are known in the East as *Ung* and *Mungul*—with the latter corresponding to the Mongols or, as Polo prefers to call them, the Tartars.

Yule finds Polo's reference here to Gog and Magog bewildering if taken at face value, and argues that the passage must instead be read as an elliptical commentary on the Wall: "Yet I think, if we read 'between the lines,' we shall see reason to believe that the Wall *was* in Polo's mind at this point of the dictation, whatever may have been his motive for withholding distincter notice of it. I cannot conceive why he should say: 'Here is what we call the country of Gog and Magog,' except as intimating 'Here we are *beside the* GREAT WALL known as the Rampart of Gog and Magog,' and being there he tries to find a reason why those names should have been applied to it."[12] If we set aside the peculiarity of Yule's claim that Polo, rather than simply discussing the Wall directly, would instead have chosen to substitute for it with a highly elliptical reference to two biblical figures who bear at most a tangential association to *another* legendary wall, he does succeed in raising a very interesting issue regarding our understanding of the identity and historicity of the Great Wall.

Yule argues that Marco Polo was using the legend of Gog and Magog to suggest an equivalence between China's Wall and what Yule calls the "Rampart of Gog and Magog." This latter is located in the narrow pass of Derbend in the Caucasus where, according to legend, Alexander the Great built an enormous iron gate to block out the "Tartars" and prevent them from invading Europe. Marco Polo himself refers to this legendary Iron Gate at another point in his text, but without mentioning the Gog/Magog connection: "Alexander caused a very strong tower to be built there, to prevent the people beyond from passing to attack him, and this got the name of the Iron Gate. This is the place that the Book of Alexander speaks of, when it tells us how he shut up the Tartars between two mountains; not that they were really Tartars, however, for there were no Tartars in those days, but they consisted of a race of people called Cominians and many besides."[13] Yule claims, in other words, that the Wall is present in Polo's text precisely as a conspicuous absence, arguing that Polo speaks here of the Gog and Magog in order to "intimate" an equivalence between China's Great Wall (which is not mentioned anywhere in Polo's text) and Alexander's Iron Gate (which Polo *does* mention, though in an unrelated section of his book).

Although Yule's argument about Polo's silent conflation of the First Emperor's Wall and Alexander's Iron Gate is probably sheer fantasy, this theory nevertheless points to the entirely plausible possibility that the legend of the Qin dynasty Wall and its successors may have helped inspire the legend of the immense iron gate that began to appear in the Alexander Romance corpus around the sixth century CE. Just as apparent cognates of *Qin* used as the name of China's first dynasty began appearing in Hindi, Greek, and Latin as early as the first and second centuries CE, it is not unreasonable to suppose that the legend of an enormous Qin Wall separating China from the Xiongnu might have made its way to Europe via Asian and Middle Eastern traders, where it could have helped provide the inspiration for a similar legendary Wall separating Europe from the Central Asian "Tartars." Furthermore, this possibility that the Qin Wall may have helped inspire the legend of the Alexandran wall centuries later and thousands of kilometers away suggestively mirrors the way in which the Ming Wall provided the catalyst for the subsequent development of the Western notion of an iconic "Great Wall of China."

This point about the potential relationship between the Qin and Alexandran walls is, of course, mere speculation. I use it here to suggest one plausible bifurcation in the tradition inspired by the original Qin dynasty, and also I use it to illustrate more generally the critical role played by these sorts of speculative processes in the constitution of the historical reality of the Wall. The vision we have inherited of the Ming Wall as the product of an unbroken historical continuity dating back to the Qin is itself, in a very real sense, the product of a continual process of (unconscious) speculation—a tradition of speculation that has gradually come to assume the status of social reality.

We find an interesting commentary on this speculative reconstruction of the Wall's origins in an essay by Borges. Inspired quite possibly by Kafka's 1917 parable about the Wall as a unity of gaps (which Borges once described as Kafka's "most memorable" work), this 1950 essay takes as its starting point the relation between the First Emperor's virtually simultaneous book-burning and wall-building projects.[14] Borges notes that these acts mirror each other quite precisely—with one attempting to erase the past and the other intended to help secure the dynasty's future. He considers several possible ways of reconciling these two visions of the First Emperor—speculating that the Qin sovereign could be seen as either "a king who began by destroying and then resigned himself to conserving, or . . . a disillusioned king who destroyed what he had previously defended"—and decides that both of these conjectures "are dramatic but lack, as far as I know, a historical basis."[15] He concludes that the Wall itself may be best approached as merely "a metaphor," in the sense that its significance lies in its symbolic, rather than its strictly material, status.

In his speculative reconstruction of the origins of the Wall, Borges is in effect applying a version of a narrative model he developed a decade earlier in another China-themed work, "The Garden of Forking Paths." This seminal story (his first to be translated into English) describes a London-based Chinese professor whose ancestor had dreamed of creating a monumental labyrinth in which "all men would lose their way."[16] This labyrinth turns out to be a novel that attempts to detail all possible futures for every present moment, yielding a "garden" of infinitely bifurcating counterfactual alternatives. In Borges's subsequent essay on the First Emperor's Wall, he presents a similar garden but in reverse—taking a concrete historical eventuality (the First Emperor's legendary acts of wall building and book burning) and working back to reconstruct all of the possible counterfactual scenarios that could explain the logical relationship between these two actions.

Beyond its relevance to Borges's fable of the Wall, this forking-garden metaphor also provides a useful model for understanding the history and historicity of the Wall. Although the Wall is frequently imagined as a paradigmatically linear entity, in reality it is characterized by a continual series of bifurcations. During the period from the Han to the Ming, for instance, the Wall's historical trajectory repeatedly branched off in different directions, as strategies of border-wall construction were appropriated by a variety of peoples and regimes positioned along the nation's northern periphery. The *symbol* of the Wall also diverged from the material structure, as the abstract ideal of a frontier Wall continued to retain significant purchase even during regimes that had no interest in building border fortifications. After the fall of the Ming an idealized vision of the Wall developed in Western discourses, largely independent of how the structure was understood back in China, and it would not be until the twentieth century that the Western and Chinese visions of the Wall would begin to reconverge.

While theoretically it would be possible to separate the Wall into each of its geographic, historical, and conceptual strands—to speak, for instance, of the Badaling section of the Ming Wall as imagined during the early twenty-first century—this approach would not accord very well with our own intuitions about what the Wall really is. We tend to imagine the Wall as a unitary and continuous entity, even while consciously recognizing the physical, historical, and conceptual specificity of its components. In practice, therefore, the Wall is generally conceived as the sum total of its individual parts—as a Borgesian garden that encompasses all of its divergent strands.

While King Hu's *Dragon Gate Inn* is positioned at a critical juncture in the Wall's history, we find another perspective on the Wall's contemporary significance if we trace one of the subsequent strands of the film itself. In 2003, the Taiwan-based director Tsai Ming-liang released an homage to King Hu's film. Entitled *Goodbye, Dragon Inn,* this recent work is structured around a screening of *Dragon Gate Inn* at Taipei's historic Fu-ho Theatre, on the eve of the theater's scheduled demolition.[17] Simultaneously reflecting on the transience of physical constructions (the theater) and the resilience of cultural productions (King Hu's film), Tsai Ming-liang's *Goodbye, Dragon Inn* explores the way in which a promise of impending destruction may provide the basis for an anticipatory sense of spectral return.

Though Tsai's homage is set in contemporary Taipei, it opens with an embedded clip of King Hu's original prologue set in Beijing. King Hu's mysterious wall circles do not appear anywhere in Tsai's homage, though two sets of suggestively similar circular wall markings had in fact begun to appear on dilapidated Beijing walls in the years leading up to the release of Tsai's film. First, in the 1990s it had become increasingly popular, in Beijing and other major Chinese cities, to mark buildings slated for demolition with the Chinese character *chai,* meaning "to demolish," circumscribed by a white circle. Second, during this same period the artist Zhang Dali began anonymously drawing white circular markings on many of those same Beijing buildings—the markings being iconic images of his own profile, which originated out of his sense of isolation and cultural alienation. Through the fortuitous coincidence of the *chai* characters and Zhang Dali's autographs, we may discern the outlines of a logic underlying the structure and function of the contemporary Wall. While the *chai* characters anticipate the imminent destruction of the buildings on whose walls they appear, Zhang Dali's graffiti, by contrast, developed out of the artist's attempt to answer his sense of cultural alienation with an anonymous assertion of identity and presence.

These intersecting themes of destruction and preservation are brought together in a popular joke that contemporary China has become a nation of *Chai-na*—literally, a nation of "demolish that." Punning on both the English word *China* and the late-nineteenth-century Japanese term for China, *Shina,* this contemporary neologism uses the same character, *na,* to render the second syllable of *China.* Although in the Japanese term this *na* was used strictly for its phonetic value, in the *Chai-na* neologism it is also used for its semantic value, as the pronoun *that. Na* belongs to a category of words linguists call "shifters," meaning that their concrete referent is contingent on the specific context in which they are uttered. We could, by extension, also see the neologism *Chai-na* as a sort of shifter—reflecting the fact that our understanding of the nation ultimately depends on the perspective from which we happen to perceive it.

The joke that China has become a nation of "demolish that" presents a version of what Foucault, in a passage discussed in Chapter 1, calls "the stark impossibility of thinking *that*." In other words, in contrast to a conventional vision of the nation as a fundamentally unified and historically continuous entity, the *Chai-na* appellation reimagines China as the product of a continual process of destruction and reconstruction. It is precisely in this challenge of attempting the impossibility of "thinking *that*," however, that we find a potential explanation for the conventional assumptions about (national) identity. In presenting the nation as a space of demolition, the *Chai-na* joke suggests a view of identity as grounded not on continuity but on a continuous process of destruction and reinvention. By a similar logic, the Wall itself could be seen as a product not so much of historical continuity and physical unity as of continuous divergence and rupture—with the identity of the Wall lying not in any single historical strand but in the collective "garden" that contains all of these intertwined "forking paths."

These contemporary mural markings, therefore, bring us back full circle to the wall circles in King Hu's film. Each set of inscriptions symbolizes the processes of destruction, transformation, and erasure that have characterized the Wall throughout its history, even as the structure's survival and resilience is ultimately predicated on these same transformative processes. It is, in other words, precisely in the Wall's ability to branch off in different directions that we find the key to its coherence as a transhistorical entity.

CHAPTER 5

Another Brick in the Wall

———

> I always feel we are encircled by a Long Wall. This Long Wall is made from old ones and has been repaired and extended with new bricks. Together, these two processes have yielded the present wall, which now encircles us all.
>
> —Lu Xun, "The Long Wall" (1925)

In 1920, the poet, writer, and political reformer Guo Moruo (whose surname, Guo, coincidentally means "outer city wall") proposed what would become one of the defining metaphors for turn-of-the-century China. Writing at the height of the May Fourth Movement, during which Chinese reformers were struggling to reassess the nation's identity following the 1911 collapse of the Qing dynasty, Guo composed a long poem entitled "Phoenix Nirvana," in which he compared the Chinese nation to the legendary bird that is reborn out of its own ashes every 500 years.[1] This poem was written against the backdrop of a contemporary debate over the fate of the nation, and the cultural tradition with which the nation had come to be identified. At issue was whether China's social and cultural legacy could be mobilized to help address the contemporary crisis, or whether it was instead necessary to discard that cultural inheritance altogether and start afresh. Some conservative figures argued for preserving those aspects of tradition that helped define China's cultural uniqueness, while others, like Guo Moruo himself, adopted an attitude of what China historian Lin Yü-sheng has labeled "totalistic anti-traditionalism"—calling for the complete overhaul of existing traditions so that new cultural and political formations might emerge, like the phoenix, from their ashes.[2]

Despite efforts to reject, "totalistically," the body of tradition China had inherited from the imperial period, it is nevertheless important to remember that the nation's 2,132-year-long span of dynastic rule had in fact never been a "totality" to begin with. Instead, this tradition could be regarded as the product of a series of gaps, interruptions, and dramatic transformations that have coalesced into an illusion of unity. By the same token, the early twentieth-century notion of totalistic *anti*-traditionalism was itself a mirage, given that earlier social and cultural traditions necessarily continued to play a crucial role in shaping the course of China's development, even as they were being repeatedly transformed to meet the needs of a new era.

The Wall is a perfect symbol of the dual process of inheritance and transformation China was undergoing during this time. The preeminent symbol of the First Emperor's unification of China, the Wall subsequently became an emblem of the emperor's tyrannical ambition. As we have seen, after the fall of the Ming, the Wall built to defend against the Mongols and Manchus lost much of its practical significance—given that the Mongols were no longer a significant threat and the Manchus had come to control all of China. It was precisely during this period, however, that discourses on the Wall's monumental significance became increasingly popular in the West, even as legends of the Qin Wall continued to circulate within China. After the fall of China's final dynasty, the Qing, this symbol of the nation's dynastic tradition did not fade into irrelevance; rather, like Guo Moruo's phoenix, it was reborn as an emblem of the new national polity that China was seeking to become.

The early twentieth-century reinvention of the Wall coincided with a profound transformation of the very notion of China. After the fall of the Qing in 1911, a republican government was established in Beijing, with Sun Yat-sen as its provisional president. Often referred to as the "father of modern China," Sun played a critical role in mapping out the administrative trajectory and political philosophy of the new republic. In a 1919 essay, Sun characterizes the Wall as "China's most famous work of land-based engineering" and describes how the First Emperor built the Wall to "safeguard the future" and "defend the nation," but then he argues that the structure not only served to help defend China against foreign attack but also played a crucial role in strengthening the nation and expanding its influence: "If we Chinese hadn't enjoyed the protection of the Long Wall, China would not have flourished and developed as it did during the Han and Tang dynasties, and would not have successfully assimilated the peoples of the south. After our country had fully developed its powers of assimilation, we were able even to assimilate our conquerors, the Mongols and the Manchus."[3] The logical progression Sun sketches here is very suggestive. He imagines the Wall as having evolved from being a defense against the northern invaders during the Qin, to facilitating the nation's expansionist assimilation of its southern neighbors during the Han and Tang, to finally enabling China's reactive assimilation of northern invaders during the Yuan and the Qing. Sun perceives the Wall, in other words, as having gone full circle from providing a defense against foreign invaders to helping transform those same invaders into Chinese subjects—after they had already succeeded in infiltrating China.

Sun Yat-sen's description of the Wall's role in facilitating the cultural assimilation of foreign invaders could be extended to China's own ability to absorb foreign values and ideas. China, needless to say, has been incorporating foreign values and ideas for millennia. At the turn of the twentieth century, the quest for cultural and intellectual assimilation began to reach a fever pitch, as reformers—humbled by the nation's defeat at the hands of the British in the first Opium War (1839–1842) and the Japanese in the first Sino-Japanese War (1894–1895)—became increasingly determined to import foreign knowledge in a wide range of areas, to strengthen the nation and reassert its position on the world stage. The result was a vast industry dedicated to translating Western and Japanese scholarship into Chinese—including not only practical works relating to technology and medicine but also a variety of political, philosophical, literary, and historical texts. The goal of many of these reformers involved a strategy of taking "Chinese learning as the basis, and Western learning as the instrument," in order to appropriate Western knowledge and technology while at the same time preserving China's cultural essence.

One of the Western concepts introduced during this turn-of-the-century period was that of an iconic "Great Wall of China." In Republican China, this image of the Wall as a national symbol encountered a very different perception of the structure as a dynastic vestige and a symbol of the First Emperor's tyrannical exploitation of the people. The resulting hybrid vision of the monument is memorably captured in a short essay by Lu Xun, a leading cultural and political figure who is frequently referred to as the "father of modern Chinese literature." Published in 1925, Lu Xun's essay combines the Chinese term *chang cheng* with a translation of the English adjective *great* (rendered here in Chinese as *weida*), to identify the Wall as a conceptually hybrid construction, a "*great* Long Wall." Lu Xun's use of the modifier *great,* moreover, is clearly sardonic, given that he actually regards the Wall as anything but great. On the contrary, he sees the structure as a symbol of infamy, or at best of futility:

> On the map, we can still find a small icon representing this construction, and just about everyone in the world who has even the least bit of education knows about it.
> In reality, however, it has never served any purpose other than to

make countless workers labor to death in vain. How could the bar-barians ever be repelled by it? Now it is but an ancient relic, yet it will never disappear entirely and therefore we must work to pre-serve it.

I always feel that we are encircled by a Long Wall. This Long Wall is made from old bricks and has been repaired and extended with new bricks. Together, these old and new bricks have yielded this wall, which now encircles everyone.

When will we stop adding new bricks to the Long Wall? This great but blasted Long Wall![4]

Starting with a strategic juxtaposition of Western and Chinese atti-tudes toward the Wall, Lu Xun then points to a contradiction at the heart of the Chinese vision of the structure, and of the cultural tra-dition it represents. Specifically, he uses the metaphor of adding new bricks to describe the way in which Chinese tradition is contin-ually changing while at the same time retaining its original conser-vative connotations. In splicing together the conventional Western and Chinese terms for the Wall, Lu Xun suggests that China's cur-rent appropriation of the West's vision of the monument could itself be seen as equivalent to merely adding a "new brick" to the existing structure—granting it another layer of meaning without fundamen-tally altering its underlying significance.

The ambivalence toward tradition revealed in Lu Xun's 1925 es-say was gradually transformed during the 1930s and 1940s, as May Fourth debates over the comparative value of tradition and moder-nity were largely displaced by China's civil war and the second Sino-Japanese War. It was precisely during this wartime period, however, that the Wall's status as a symbol of tradition and innova-tion began to undergo a critical transformation within China itself. We may approach the Wall's transformation during this period by first turning to another transcendental symbol of national iden-tity—the Long March.

The Long March began in 1934, when several divisions of the Red Army found themselves cornered in southern Jiangxi Province by Chiang Kai-shek's Nationalist forces, but managed to escape by following a broad, northwesterly loop across difficult terrain that eventually brought them to their new base camp in Yan'an, in northern Shaanxi Province. In practical terms, the Long March was a virtual disaster, with fewer than 10 percent of the 100,000 soldiers who left Jiangxi making it to Yan'an alive. On a symbolic level, however, the march constituted a crucial victory for the besieged Communist forces, and would come to crystallize their long and complicated road toward political unification in 1949. The Long March also marked an important step in the subsequent rise to power of Mao Zedong, who personally led the First Red Army out of Jiangxi, just as the hardship endured by the soldiers who managed to survive the trek helped to cement their loyalty to one another and to the Party, and their bravery and perseverance earned them the respect of the peasants who would subsequently become some of the Party's most important constituents.

The Long March has become one of the most emotionally resonant symbols of the unification of modern China, despite the fact that, like the Wall, the march was hardly a unitary entity to begin with. What we now regard as the Long March actually includes several discrete sets of troop movements as the First, Third, and Fourth Red Armies followed three distinct routes out of Jiangxi. It goes without saying, furthermore, that the ordeal must have been experienced very differently by each of the tens of thousands of soldiers who participated in it. When a couple of political scientists from Harvard and Yale interviewed several of the Long March survivors half a century after the fact, they found that virtually all of the former soldiers initially provided descriptions of the march that hewed closely to the standard historical account. It was only after the researchers pressed their informants on apparently incongruous details in their stories that the soldiers began to modify their accounts, which allowed disparate perspectives on the event to emerge and thereby transforming the putatively unitary Long March into a cluster of separate "long marches."[5]

As the Long March was under way, the playwright Tian Han penned the lyrics to another "march"—the song known in English as "The March of the Volunteers." Tian Han originally wrote the lyrics in 1934 as part of a poem entitled "Ten-thousand-*li*-long Long Wall" for a play he was working on, though it was subsequently rumored that he actually composed the song on strips of tobacco paper while imprisoned in a Chinese Nationalist Party jail the following year. Regardless of the precise circumstances of the work's composition, the appearance of the final stanza of the Long Wall poem in a climactic scene in Xu Xingzhi's 1935 film *Sons and Daughters in Troubled Times* set the stage for its subsequent fame as one of the most important songs of twentieth-century China.[6]

Sons and Daughters focuses on a young poet by the name of Xin Baihua, who is nicknamed the "Great Wall poet." Baihua and his friend Liang Zhifu live upstairs from a young woman named Ah Feng and her mother, and after Ah Feng's mother dies, Baihua and Zhifu sell their own furniture to help Ah Feng pay her rent and sponsor her education. When Ah Feng visits the young men in their room upstairs one day, she notices a painting of a phoenix on the wall, and Xin Baihua recounts—using language strikingly similar to that of Guo Moruo's 1920 "Phoenix Nirvana" poem—the legend of the phoenix that immolates itself every five hundred years and is then reborn from its own ashes. Ah Feng is so taken with this legend that she immediately decides to change her name from Ah Feng, which could be translated as "little phoenix," to Xinfeng —literally, "new phoenix." Ah Feng/Xinfeng subsequently moves away to join a revolutionary dance troop and Liang Zhifu is arrested for his revolutionary activities. Xin Baihua is nearly arrested as well, but he manages to escape thanks to the assistance of a rich widow, with whom he becomes romantically involved. After being released from jail, Liang Zhifu joins the Red Army and is eventually killed on the battlefield; in his final letter to Xin Baihua he entreats his friend, "Please do not give up your responsibility to defend the Great Wall just for a woman."

Xin Baihua eventually heeds his friend's advice and leaves the widow to join the struggle against the Japanese, and the film concludes with his joyful reunion with the politically progressive Xinfeng. The final scene depicts them marching together against the Japanese while defiantly singing "March of the Volunteers":

> Arise, ye who refuse to be slaves;
> With our very flesh and blood, let us build our new Long Wall!
> The people of China are at their most critical time,
> Everybody must roar defiance
> Arise! Arise! Arise!
> The masses are of one mind,
> Brave the enemy's gunfire,
> March on! March on! March on!

This appeal to the Wall as a symbol for nation building is played out in the film against the erotically charged reunion of Xin Baihua and Xinfeng, and their sublimated romantic desire functions as a foil for their revolutionary ardor and nationalist passion. More abstractly, the song's call to build a "new" Long Wall reflects not only an interest in forging a new nation but also the revolutionary transformation that the concept of the Wall was undergoing during this same period.

The Wall's reinvention as a revolutionary and nationalistic icon was sanctified a decade and a half later when Mao Zedong selected Tian Han's "March of the Volunteers"—set to a melody by the composer Nie Er—as the national anthem of the nascent People's Republic of China. The result, however, could be compared with the Qin anthem that Gao Jianli composed for the 2006 opera *The First Emperor* (discussed in Chapter 2), in which the anthem's patriotic purpose is silently subverted by its incorporation of a protest song sung by slaves building the Wall. What is curious about Mao's selection of "March of the Volunteers" as the PRC's new anthem, however, is that it actually makes no mention of Mao, Maoism, or any of the specific ideological elements with which Mao's China would come to be identified.

Through a quirk of fate, the anthem's implicit "betrayal" of the PRC's Maoist ideals was figuratively redressed when Tian Han was imprisoned during the Cultural Revolution for alleged antirevolutionary activities, resulting in the unofficial proscription of his "March of the Volunteers." For several years, the much more explicitly Maoist "The East Is Red"—which begins, "The east is red, the sun is rising. China has brought forth a Mao Zedong"—was used as the nation's de facto anthem, although the state constitution was never formally amended to reflect the change. In 1978, two years after the death of Mao and the official end of the Cultural Revolution, Nie Er's melody to the original anthem was rehabilitated, although accompanied by a new set of explicitly Communist lyrics (which begin, "March on, people of all heroic nationalities! The great Communist Party leads us in continuing the Long March"). Among other things, these lyrics replaced the original reference to the Long Wall in "March of the Volunteers" (". . . let us build our new Long Wall!") with an allusion to the Long March (". . . leads us in continuing the Long March"). This substitution reflects not only prosodic considerations—in Chinese, "long march" (pronounced *cháng zhēng*) and "long wall" (pronounced *cháng chéng*) are almost precise homophones, with the "ch" in *cheng* being simply an aspirated version of the retroflex "zh" in *zheng*—but furthermore reflects the intimate connection between the Wall and the March in the Chinese collective imagination. Both were monumental endeavors that were the product of the collective effort of hundreds of thousands of men, and both have helped provide the ideological foundation for modern China.

The Wall passes just north of the Yan'an area where the Communists set up their new base camp at the end of the Long March, and it was this geographic proximity to Yan'an that inspired Mao in 1935 to write a short poem entitled "Mount Liupan," offering encouragement to the First Red Army as it was approaching its destination. The poem begins:

> The sky is high, the clouds are pale,
> We watch as the wild geese disappear southward.
> If we fail to reach the Long Wall, we are not true men,
> We who have marched more than twenty thousand *li*.[7]

Mao's allusion to the twenty thousand *li* the Red Army is credited with having covered evokes a sense of a vast distance, but it also resonates with the ten-thousand *li* length traditionally attributed to the Long Wall. If we consider the length of the Long March more literally, meanwhile, additional interesting parallels with the Long Wall emerge. When British researchers recently retraced the First Army's route, for instance, they found that the distance the army had covered was actually closer to six thousand kilometers, or just slightly over ten thousand *li* (five thousand kilometers)—meaning that, through an odd quirk of fate, the distance covered during the Long March was roughly comparable to the (reputed) length of the Qin dynasty's original Long Wall (not to mention the roughly six-thousand-kilometer length of the extant Ming Wall).[8]

Even as Mao's poem riffed on Sima Qian's famous ten-thousand-*li*-long formulation, it also inspired a phrase that has become almost as closely associated with the Wall as Sima Qian's own. Although the third line of the poem technically should be translated, "If *we* fail to *reach* the Wall, we will *not be real men*" in contemporary usage it is generally rendered as, "If *you* haven't been to the Wall, *you* are not a real man." In Chinese, the poem contains no personal pronouns, and because Chinese verbs are not conjugated, the subject and addressee must therefore be extrapolated from the context. Whereas in the original work Mao was clearly addressing his Red Army troops, if the line is read in isolation it could be understood as referring to *anyone*.

The syntactic indeterminacy of the subject in this line is mirrored by a semantic ambiguity in the nominative clause at the end. Mao uses the term *hao han,* which in colloquial usage means essentially "good fellow" and carries heroic connotations. If broken down into its individual characters, however, the term could also be seen as having rather different overtones, given that *Han* is the same character used to refer to contemporary China's dominant ethnic group. The first dynasty to officially divide the population into protoethnic categories was the Yuan, which recognized four such categories: the Mongols, the Semu, which included a variety of other non-Mongol pastoral peoples, and the Northern and Southern Han. Ethnic distinctions became increasingly formalized during the Ming and Qing, while the PRC currently maintains a strict taxonomical system wherein every citizen is assigned to one of fifty-six different ethnicities—with more than 90 percent of the population belonging to the Han ethnicity. One result of this latter policy is that it allows the nation to celebrate its ethnic plurality while implicitly reinforcing the equation of Chineseness with Han identity—using a token recognition of ethnic distinctiveness to reaffirm the normative character of Han identity. Mao was using, in other words, a colloquial term that carries partially effaced ethnic connotations, while the very effacement of those connotations anticipated Maoist China's subsequent attempts to formalize and naturalize a vision of national identity.

While the Wall is often imagined as a barrier between different ethnic or protoethnic groups (for example, the Han and the Xiongnu, the Han and the Mongols, the Manchu and the Han), in practice it has more often functioned as a symptom of an intimate *interrelationship* between groups, and of the wall-builders' own process of Sinicization. Just as Sun Yat-sen argued in 1919 that the

Wall could be seen as a tool of ethnic assimilation, Mao's "if we fail to reach" line could be read as implying that the mere act of reaching the Wall rendered the subject ethnically "Han."

In contrast to Mao's treatment of the Wall as a goal or destination, leftist director Yuan Muzhi, in his classic film *Street Angel*, cites the Wall as a symbol of displacement.[9] Released in 1937, just two years after Mao penned his "Mount Liupan" poem, the film focuses on two sisters who have fled war-ravaged Manchuria and are now working as singsong girls in a Shanghai teahouse. One of the first scenes of the film depicts the younger of the sisters being forced to perform for some lecherous customers. As the girl, Xiao Hong, sings a tune called "Song of Four Seasons," the camera repeatedly cuts back and forth between shots of her tear-stained face and a montage of scenic images, concluding with an image of the Wall that coincides with the song's allusion to the legend of Lady Meng Jiang:

> Winter comes and snow flurries down.
> When winter clothes are ready I'll send them to my man.
> The long wall built of blood and flesh is long.
> Would that I could be the ancient Meng Jiang.

Xiao Hong appropriates a version of Tian Han's metaphor of the Wall as a product of flesh and blood ("with our very flesh and blood, let us build our new Long Wall") and transforms it into an emblem of subjugation and confinement ("the long wall built of blood and flesh is long"). The shots of the snow-covered stone Wall that accompany this allusion to Lady Meng Jiang suggest that the structure symbolizes the Manchurian homeland to which Xiao Hong yearns to return.

Although *Street Angel* does not refer again to the Wall after this initial scene, it does feature another distinctive wall. One of Xiao Hong's friends is a semiliterate newspaper peddler who has plastered the walls of his cramped, ramshackle apartment with old newspapers. In Republican China, print media such as journals and newspapers provided a crucial conduit for the introduction of "modern" knowledge and values, though the newspaper peddler and his companions derive little benefit from this modernization process. Instead, they literally surround themselves with newsprint, occasionally trying to find inspiration in the isolated words or phrases contained in the clippings. In this way, the papered walls of the apartment symbolize the structural limits on the characters' social mobility, as well as their dreams of liberation.

Another version of this sort of "text wall" can be found in another movie set in the same 1930s period, but filmed more than half a century later. Directed by Ching Siu-tung, who also directed *Fight and Love with a Terracotta Warrior*, the 1996 martial arts fantasy *Dr. Wai in "The Scripture with No Words"* features an author named Chow Si-kit (played by Jet Li), who is working on a serialized novel about a 1930s adventurer and archaeologist known as Dr. Wai (also played by Jet Li).[10] The film opens with Chow undergoing a stressful divorce that has literally emptied out his "idea box" (a small wooden box in which he places his notes for the upcoming serial) and left him stricken with a debilitating case of writer's block. Fortunately, a couple of coworkers provide him with a new plotline revolving around a quest for a "wordless scripture" believed to hold the secrets of the "future of the people," together with the scripture's sacred sutra box (which had recently been unearthed by the Japanese from an excavation site in Sichuan). Chow picks up this narrative thread and increasingly comes to identify with the quest of his Indiana Jones–style protagonist. Once Dr. Wai, in the embedded narrative, finally recovers the sutra box, he takes it to the Wall, where it causes an entire section of the structure to collapse. Inside the Wall he finds a bone-strewn cavern containing the wordless scripture, and after he places the document in its sacred box, he then (slipping back into his original persona as the contemporary author) asks it whether he will ever see his wife again. The scripture responds by projecting an image of Chow and his wife (in the present) on the inner surface of the Wall, whereupon the film abruptly jumps back to the present day and shows Chow reconciling with his wife.

In this way, the quest for the wordless scripture comes full circle. What begins as the author's personal struggle with his marital difficulties is reimagined as a nationalistic quest to find a sacred document containing the key to the "future of the people," and then reverts back at the end to its original focus on Chow's relationship with his wife. While this moment of historical return is literally set against the backdrop of the Wall, the film also simultaneously presents a vision of the historicity of the Wall. Just as Chow/Wai sees an image of his (Chow's) own personal desires and aspirations projected on the inner surface of the Wall, the Wall often functions as a virtual screen onto which viewers may project their respective hopes and ideals.

Dr. Wai's quest for a wordless scripture is partially inspired by the Ming dynasty novel *Journey to the West*.[11] Based on the seventh-century monk Xuanzang's journey to India to retrieve Buddhist sutras, the novel teams the monk (known in English translation as Tripitaka) with the irascible Monkey King and two other anthropomorphic disciples, who join him on his journey to "the West." After countless trials and tribulations, the pilgrims finally arrive at their destination and obtain the desired texts, but as they are on their way back home they discover that they have been given a bundle of blank pages. Indignant, they return to the Buddhist Patriarch, who responds with a chuckle, "Since you people came with empty hands to acquire scriptures, blank texts were handed over to you. But these blank texts are actually true, wordless scriptures, and they are just as good as those with words. However, those creatures in your Land of the East are so foolish and unenlightened that I have no choice but to impart to you now the texts with words."[12]

The Patriarch argues that the highest truth is beyond words, suggesting that the literal meaning of the text is secondary to the uses to which the text is put. In a similar spirit, the significance of *Journey to the West* itself may be seen as lying not so much in the actual contents of the work but rather in the ways in which the narrative has been used in different contexts. One of China's best-loved novels, the narrative has captured the imagination of everyone from children to Buddhist scholars and has inspired a wide variety of sequels and adaptations, ranging from late-imperial sequels like *A Ridiculous Journey to the West,* to a 2001 U.S. television miniseries about an American businessman who is magically transported back to late-Ming China to rescue the original text of the novel and save civilization as we know it. This eclectic range of readings and adaptations suggests that the ultimate significance of the narrative lies not in its content, but in the way in which it provides a figurative screen against which the concerns and anxieties of each age may be projected.

Just as *Journey to the West* has functioned as a figurative "wordless scripture" or blank screen throughout its history, the Wall has similarly been repeatedly rebuilt and transformed to meet each era's shifting needs and concerns. To the extent that essays, songs, poems, and films illustrate the gradual rehabilitation, during the first half of the century, of the Wall's significance in China, for instance, a series of governmental directives and private initiatives reflect a parallel interest, during the latter half of the century, in restoring the physical structure itself. In 1952, the poet-turned-bureaucrat Guo Moruo—in his new capacity as vice premier of the State Council and chair of the Committee on Culture and Education—laid out the first modern proposal to reconstruct the Wall. Implicitly building on his earlier description of new China as a phoenix rising from its own ashes, Guo Moruo called for the Badaling section of the Wall outside Beijing to be thoroughly repaired and restored to a semblance of its former glory. This project was completed five years later, in 1957, whereupon the renovated section of the Wall was officially opened to the public. Badaling has since become one of China's biggest attractions, and an estimated 130 million visitors have made the pilgrimage to see it since it reopened in 1957.

In addition to being a tourist site, Badaling is also a required stop for foreign leaders and other dignitaries, as we have seen. In 1972, for instance, U.S. president Richard Nixon visited Badaling during his historic visit to China, where he made his famous "a great wall . . . built by a great people" pronouncement:

> And one stands there and sees the wall going to the peak of this mountain and realizes it runs for hundreds of miles—as a matter of fact, thousands of miles—over the mountains and through the valleys of this country [and] that it was built over 2,000 years ago. I think that you have to conclude that this is a great wall and it had to be built by a great people. It is certainly a symbol of what China in the past has been and what China in the future can become. A people that could build a wall like this certainly [has] a great past to be proud of. And a people that have this kind of a past must also have a great future.[13]

Nixon's emphasis on the Wall's "great"-ness proves eminently infectious, spilling out beyond the confines of the Wall and coloring everything with which the structure is associated—including the people who constructed it, the historical past out of which it emerged, and even the future into which it is headed. Just as Lu Xun used the same adjective in arguing that the Wall was actually anything but "great," the very repetition in Nixon's emphasis on how everything relating to the Wall is "great" points to an inescapable chasm at the heart of our vision of the structure.

An uncanny echo of Nixon's 1972 visit to the Wall took place seventeen years later, when Mikhail Gorbachev made the first visit to China by a Soviet leader in thirty years. In contrast to the small army of reporters who followed Nixon's every move, media coverage of the Soviet president's trip was overshadowed by the 1989

Tiananmen Square pro-democracy protests that were going on at the time he arrived. Gorbachev did, however, manage to make the requisite trip to Badaling, where he famously remarked, "It's a very beautiful work, but there are already too many walls between people." A reporter then asked him the logical follow-up question: whether this meant he (whom Ronald Reagan, during a trip to Berlin two years earlier, had challenged to "tear down this wall!") would allow the Berlin Wall—that most infamous of cold war symbols—to be dismantled, to which the leader of the soon-to-be-defunct Soviet Union replied, "Why not?"

Why not, indeed. On November 9, 1989, just months after Gorbachev's trip to Beijing, the Berlin Wall became a political relic as tens of thousands of East Germans rushed through in response to a premature announcement by Günter Schabowski, the East German minister of propaganda, that the militarized border was to be opened up. Stunned by the wave of humanity, the East German guards held their fire and allowed their compatriots to pass through to West Germany. Although it would take several more months for the political restrictions on movement between East and West Germany to be officially lifted, and even longer for the physical wall itself to be dismantled, that November afternoon is remembered as the day the Berlin Wall fell.

In contrast to the fascination in the 1980s with whether and when the Berlin Wall would be brought down, discussions of China's Wall during the same period tended to focus on the inverse question of how to *restore* the monument to its presumptive greatness. Although Badaling had been carefully repaired and maintained, much of the rest of the structure had been ravaged by erosion and general neglect, and in many regions locals had torn it down to reuse its bricks for their own constructions. Adding insult to injury, during the Cultural Revolution (1966–1976) the Wall had been a target of the "Attack the Four Olds" campaign, which promoted concerted action against old customs, culture, habits, and ideas carried over from pre-1949 China. In 1984, in response to the Wall's physical and symbolic deterioration, Deng Xiaoping—the de facto leader of China at that point—launched a campaign to "love our country and restore the Great Wall." Echoing Guo Moruo's 1952 five-year plan to rebuild the Badaling section of the Wall, Deng's 1984 campaign called for the physical restoration of specific sections, and an aggressive refurbishing of the public's *vision* of the structure. The goal of the campaign was not merely to (re)affirm the monument's significance as a transhistorical symbol of the nation but also to reaffirm the strength and majesty of the nation itself.

Deng Xiaoping's 1984 "restore the Great Wall" campaign helped set in motion a process of restoration and rehabilitation that continues today. In 1987, for instance, China founded the Great Wall Society, which has developed into the most prominent Chinese-led Wall-preservation group; also that same year the United Nations Educational, Scientific, and Cultural Organization (UNESCO) designated several sections of the Wall as official World Heritage Sites —including Badaling, near Beijing; Jiayuguan, in far-western Gansu Province; and Shanhaiguan, where the Wall reaches the Gulf of Bohai. This also happened to be the year that William Lindesay, the future founder of the international Wall-preservation society Friends of the Great Wall, first visited the Wall.

In 2002 the World Monuments Fund added the Wall to its list of the world's 100 most endangered sites. Technically speaking, the Wall itself was not listed but rather the "Cultural Landscape of the Great Wall, Beijing Region." In practical terms, this specification of the Wall's "cultural landscape" was intended to encourage the preservation of the geographic region through which the Wall runs—to limit, for instance, new construction in the immediate vicinity of the Wall that would have an impact on its appearance and people's perception of it. At the same time, however, this emphasis on the Wall's cultural landscape speaks more generally to the actual context within which it is perceived and understood. It is this abstract landscape, in turn, that permits us to see the physical structure—which is the product of a continual process of erosion, destruction, renovation, and reconstruction—as being what Lindesay calls in a different context a "continuity of the wall." It is precisely the existence of this abstract cultural landscape that allows us to perceive the Wall as an unbroken "continuity"—but specifically as a continuous process of transformation and reinvention.

Ironically, even as the various initiatives to help preserve the Wall are under way, the precise condition of the structure being "preserved" remains rather unclear. For a long time there had been a surprising dearth of reliable surveys of the structure, though in 2007 China's State Administration of Cultural Heritage and State Bureau of Surveying and Mapping initiated a four-year project using a combination of global positioning system (GPS) and infrared technologies that was billed as the first comprehensive survey of the entire structure. The results of the first half of the survey, focusing on the Ming Wall, were released in the spring of 2009, and they included an announcement of the discovery of several hundred kilometers of previously undocumented stretches of the Ming Wall in regions ranging from Liaoning Province in the east to the Jiayuguan region in the far west; they also revealed that the overall length of the Wall had been measured at 8,851.8 kilometers, more than two thousand kilometers longer than had been expected. As with the archaeologist Jing Ai's hyperprecise historical calculations of the Wall's length (discussed in Chapter 1), the survey's attempts to specify the Wall's length down to the nearest tenth of a meter suggests an overcompensatory response to an underlying anxiety about the very possibility of measuring the Wall at all. Even setting aside questions of how much of the historical structure must be present in order to be considered extant, the survey's specification that more than a quarter of the revised length (2,232.5 kilometers, to be exact) didn't consist of walls at all but of natural defensive barriers, such as hills and rivers (together with an additional 359.7 kilometers of trenches), brings into question how we understand the very nature of the Wall.

Even as this official survey was celebrating the radical *expansion* of the known Wall as previously understood, the Chinese government was simultaneously attempting to significantly *restrict* access to most of the Wall. Regulations prohibiting visitors from traveling to parts of the Wall outside designated tourist sections are ostensibly intended to help preserve the rapidly deteriorating structure from further damage, though in practice they also have the effect of further delimiting the actual vision that most visitors will have of the famous monument. Sometimes referred to as the "wild wall," the unrestored sections both undergird and undermine the structure as we have come to know it. Inaccessible to casual tourists and invisible in most standard representations of the structure, this wild wall provides a silent reminder of the perpetual process of destruction and reconstruction on which the Wall's current significance is necessarily predicated.

Another way of approaching these questions of the Wall's identity would be to consider the structure as a hybrid of the figures of Monkey in *Journey to the West* and the phoenix in Guo Moruo's 1920 poem. That is to say, the Wall may be seen as either having enjoyed a basically continuous existence from antiquity to the present, like Monkey, or as having repeatedly been destroyed and figuratively reborn, like the phoenix. This view of the Wall as a hybrid of the figures of Monkey and the phoenix highlights a curious parallel between the two legends. Just as Guo Moruo's phoenix is reborn every 500 years, Monkey's and Tripitaka's "journey to the West" begins only after Monkey has been released from his 500-year incarceration beneath the Mountain of Five Phases. The two texts, however, diverge in their understanding of the significance of this semimillennial return—with the phoenix being imagined as the product of a cycle of destruction and rebirth, while Monkey is viewed as having reawakened essentially unchanged after a long dormancy. Meanwhile, the Wall (the Ming dynasty incarnation of which coincidentally happens to be approximately five hundred years old) may be viewed as a synthesis of these two models—as an entity that has been repeatedly destroyed and reborn while also being defined by its capacity for fragmentation and transformation.

In the figures of Monkey and the phoenix, therefore, we find a different version of the models of identity and reference identified, in Chapter 1, as antidescriptive and descriptive, and compared metaphorically, in Chapter 2, to the figures of Zhang Yimou's warrior and Gong Li's starlet in *Fight and Love with a Terracotta Warrior*. As I have suggested, these two models are not directly opposed to each other but are instead complementary. We find a different perspective on this complementarity if we turn to another aspect of the legends of Monkey and the phoenix. While one of Monkey's most distinctive skills is his ability to take hairs from his body and transform them into miniature replicas of himself, Guo Moruo's phoenix/*fenghuang* is the product of two distinct mythological traditions (Egyptian and Chinese), even as the traditional Chinese *fenghuang* is itself a composite of a variety of distinct avian species. Seen as a synthesis of these two figures, therefore, the Wall is the product of a process of continual fragmentation and consolidation, a hybrid of distinct elements that are constantly threatening to dissolve back into individual fragments. By this logic, our ability to perceive the Wall as possessing a stable and unitary identity is made possible by the fact that the symbolic core of that identity is a protean construct that is constantly being reinvented and reimagined.

The Wall, in other words, may be perceived as a historically continuous and conceptually unified entity (like the proverbial Monkey) insofar as its identity is actually grounded on a phoenix-like core that is in a constant state of transformation. What permits us to perceive the Wall as a coherent and singular entity is the fact that in actuality it is neither coherent nor singular. The monument's hybrid and multifaceted character permits it to transform itself over time, while simultaneously allowing observers to perceive it as the sort of conceptual unity that meets their particular needs. The primary constant throughout the Wall's history, accordingly, is precisely its *lack* of constancy, and it is that protean quality that figuratively holds the structure together.

CHAPTER 6

A Very Queer Thing

———

If there is anything which modern China can safely be assumed to regard with respect and devotion it is that famous wall, so ancient, so useless, so queer, and so inconvenient.

—*New York Times,* June 28, 1899

The Wall, as Marx might have said, is a very queer thing. At first sight it appears easily understood, but upon closer analysis it is revealed to be really quite odd, abounding in metaphysical subtleties. Part of the reason for the Wall's peculiarity lies in the fact that in addition to being a concrete, physical artifact, it is also an abstract repository of cultural value. This symbolic dimension, furthermore, flows across the same national and conceptual borders of which the Wall is a preeminent icon, and it is this fungibility that permits the Wall to circulate throughout an increasingly globalized world.

This conjunction of solidity and mobility is nicely captured in a description—in a remarkable 1981 novel by Chinese émigré author Hualing Nieh—of a snow globe containing a miniature replica of the Wall.[1] In the book, this tourist trinket is a memento of the protagonist's Chinese homeland, and symbolizes the intractable psychological walls she has drawn up between her pre- and post-immigrant selves. A snow globe is, of course, a glass or plastic sphere containing a miniature representation of a snow-swept scene. The scene may be imaginary, as in the ubiquitous Christmas

globes we see during the holiday season, or it may be a representation of an actual landmark like the Wall. As a conveniently portable
emblem of a real or imaginary site, a snow globe exemplifies a process of globalization (or what in this context we might call *snow-
globalization*): the transformation of local identity into a set of free-
floating commodities within an increasingly globalized symbolic
economy. Nieh's miniature Wall, therefore, presents a wonderfully
apt image of a hermetically enclosed structure that is itself a quintessential symbol of both boundaries and boundlessness. It is this
fantasy of being able to reduce the vast Wall to a palm-size artifact,
furthermore, that underlies the perennial fascination with the possibility of viewing the Wall from outer space—which is to say, of seeing the structure positioned against the backdrop of the terrestrial
globe.

A cofounder of the University of Iowa's critically acclaimed International Writing Program, Hualing Nieh immigrated to the United
States in 1964 from China, via Taiwan, and her 1981 novel *Mulberry and Peach* describes the culture shock that can result from
this sort of transnational displacement. Like Nieh, the work's protagonist is a Chinese woman who has relocated to the United States
from China via Taiwan; the Mulberry and Peach in the title refer
to the two distinct personas into which the protagonist's identity
fractures as she struggles to adapt to her new environment. Her
Peach identity corresponds to the fiery and aggressive personality
that emerges after she arrives in the United States, while the name
Mulberry denotes the now-suppressed demure personality associated with her earlier existence in China. The miniature Wall inside
Peach's snow globe thus represents her attempts to seal off her own
earlier identity, even as the presence of the snow globe in Peach's life
testifies to the degree to which her earlier Chinese identity continues
to intrude into her contemporary, immigrant one. More generally,
the snow globe speaks to the politics of individual identity in an increasingly transnational era, to the processes of commoditization

that accompany these same transnational circuits, and to the way the actual stone Wall has been systematically repackaged as a sterile symbol of "Chineseness" in the modern world.

One of the cornerstones of Marxist theory on which both the Chinese Communist Party and the People's Republic are grounded involves a critique of capitalism's role in reducing commodities to the status of abstract repositories of value, thereby eliding the physical human labor that was responsible for their production in the first place. This interrogation of the relationship between concrete labor and abstract value is ironically played out in the Wall's own transformation from a symbol of the First Emperor's exploitative tyranny into a token of exchange within the contemporary global economy. In view of Marxism's commitment to reaffirming the underlying labor value of material commodities, it is curious that it was China's Communist regime that helped strip the Wall of its traditional connotations of exploited labor and refashioned it into a quintessential commodity in its own right—a symbol of the cosmopolitan nation that China is striving to become.

Even in its status as a national icon, the Wall has undergone a similar reversal from a symbol of (Communist) China to an emblem of the capitalist order against which China has ostensibly attempted to position itself. The result of this latter transformation can be seen not only in the vast tourist industry that has developed around the monument but also in the tendency among Chinese corporations to use the Wall in their name or logo. In 1924, for instance, one of Shanghai's first film studios was named after the Wall, and in the late 1940s the same name was adopted by one of Hong Kong's leading leftist film studios, which was well known for its patriotism toward Mainland China. More recently, it has also been borrowed for the name of an aerospace corporation, a cargo airline established by that same corporation, and an automobile company that, in 2008, became the first private Chinese auto company to be listed on the Hong Kong Stock Exchange. The Wall has been used in the name of a Chinese life insurance company, and as the logo of a major credit card issued by the Bank of China. Perhaps the clearest illustration of the Wall's commodification, however, can be found in the structure's long and complicated association with Chinese currency, culminating in its appearance on the back of many of China's current one-yuan bills. A nation's currency is one of the preeminent symbols of its identity, as well as one of its primary points of contact with the rest of the world, and accordingly the Wall's appearance on China's one-yuan notes underscores the monument's emergence as a globally recognized symbol of China itself.

The yuan, modern China's basic unit of currency, came into use at the end of the nineteenth century, when it was established to provide a domestic equivalent to the Mexican silver dollars that had become the de facto national standard. Even after the fall of the Qing dynasty in 1911, China's new republican government and many of its provincial governments continued minting yuan coins and paper money. By the 1940s, there were several competing versions of the yuan in use in China, including the banknotes printed by the Nationalist government, those used in the Communist-controlled "soviets" in southern Jiangxi and surrounding areas, and those issued by the occupying Japanese forces (the Japanese yen is rendered with a version of the same ideograph used to refer to the Chinese yuan). The end of the Sino-Japanese War in 1945 did little to stabilize the nation's monetary system, and over the next two years the Nationalist yuan plummeted in value from 20 yuan to the dollar to more than 73,000 to the dollar. Five-hundred-yuan notes were introduced in 1946, followed by 10,000-yuan notes two years later, though by that point the currency had already become so devalued that it reportedly cost the government 7,000 yuan to print each 10,000-yuan note, and many consumers were forced to use stacks of bank notes bound together into what were known as "cash bricks" in lieu of the nearly worthless individual bills.

Near the nadir of this hyperinflationary cash-brick economy, the

Great Wall Bank (or Bank of Chang Chung, as it was rendered in the transliteration system used at the time) was established as the central bank in the Communist-controlled Hebei-Rehe-Liaoning Liberated Area in the north, and it began printing currency with an image of the Great Wall on the back of each bill. The bank's appeal to the symbol of the Wall, however, provided scant defense against the waves of inflation that continued to rock the economy, and by September 1948 the value of the yuan had fallen by yet another order of magnitude, to around 20 million yuan to the dollar. Less than a year later the Communists finally prevailed in their civil conflict with the Nationalists, and—in an echo of the First Emperor's standardization of the nation's currency two thousand years earlier—one of Chairman Mao's first actions after founding the PRC was to phase out all of the wartime banks and replace them with the new state-run People's Bank of China. The obsolete wartime notes could be exchanged for new yuan bills at rates ranging from virtual parity up to 5,000 to 1 (the Great Wall Bank's own former currency, for instance, was valued at a rate of 2,000 to 1).

In minting its new currency, the PRC was attempting to wipe clean the preceding period of economic chaos, and over the next couple of decades it would go to considerable effort to reinvent China's overall economic policy. Under the PRC's planned economy, many staples and other commodities could be acquired only with ration coupons, just as state enterprises were managed based on government directives rather than strict market considerations. Despite the government's attempts to maintain almost absolute control over economic matters, however, the nation's currency continued to suffer from extraordinary inflationary pressures, to the point that the central bank was ultimately forced, on January 1, 1970, to remove the radically devalued *renminpiao* (literally, "people's bills," as the yuan notes were technically called) from circulation and replace them—at a virtual cash-brick rate of 10,000 to 1—with "people's currency," the *renminbi* (RMB) that are still in use today. The value of the new RMB was initially pegged to the U.S. dollar, but when the value of the dollar plummeted in 1972, the government shifted the standard to the Hong Kong dollar, and then in 1974 it shifted it again to an undisclosed basket of foreign currencies. However, regardless of whether the basis of the new RMB yuan was the U.S. dollar, the Hong Kong dollar, or a collection of foreign currencies, China's attempts to stabilize its currency by shielding it from the foreign exchange market paradoxically relied on a parallel effort to link the yuan to the same foreign currencies against which the government was trying to protect itself.

Following Chairman Mao's death and the official end of the Cultural Revolution in 1976, the door was opened for new leadership and an attendant shift in economic policy. In 1978, Mao's de facto successor, Deng Xiaoping, inaugurated the Reform and Opening-Up Campaign, which imposed a series of political and market reforms to help the nation transition into what Deng euphemistically called "socialism with Chinese characteristics." This campaign was the catalyst for a period of remarkable economic expansion, including several multiyear stretches of double-digit annual growth. Even as the government was attempting to open up China's economy, however, it was simultaneously establishing new measures in an attempt to safeguard the economy from foreign influence. Because the RMB was not directly convertible with foreign currency, for instance, in 1980 the central bank established a special currency known as Foreign Exchange Certificates (FEC), which were nominally equivalent to the domestic RMB but had a significantly higher value on the black market. Intended to encourage tourism, FEC could be purchased by foreigners and used to buy a variety of imported commodities that the government did not wish to make available to the population as a whole. Conceived as a way of maintaining the RMB's status as a barrier protecting the nation's domestic economy from foreign influence, the FEC notes actually helped facilitate the entry into China of foreign capital and capitalism.

In the context of these attempts to open up the nation's economy to foreign trade while shielding it from outside influence, in 1988 China's central bank began issuing its fourth series of currency. Each of the one-yuan bills in this new series featured an image of the Wall on one side and (like the bills of other denominations in the series) a picture of ethnic minority women on the other. The government backdated the bills to 1980, and they remain legal tender today (though a fifth series of notes, sans Wall, was introduced in 2004). The irony, however, is that even as China's basic unit of currency featured a symbol of national boundaries, its economy was becoming increasingly intertwined with the global economy. China attempted to hold the value of the yuan steady, but as the nation's trade surplus continued to balloon in the 2000s, the central bank found it necessary to keep increasing its foreign-currency reserves in order to stabilize the yuan, which meant that the stability of the nation's *domestic* currency was being preserved through the introduction of a vast sum of *foreign* capital. In March of 2010, the value of those foreign reserves stood at almost two and a half trillion dollars, of which approximately a third was in the form of U.S.-government bonds—making China by far the largest servicer of America's national debt.

Deng's Reform and Opening-Up Campaign coincided with a series of transformations in China's political and artistic culture. One of the pivotal political developments during this period, for instance, was the emergence of the so-called Xidan Democracy Wall. In November 1978, protesters began posting "big character posters" on a low brick wall along a busy street west of Tiananmen Square. These texts addressed a variety of sensitive political topics, ranging from Chairman Mao and the recently concluded Cultural Revolution to more immediate concerns such as Deng Xiaoping's ongoing reforms. One of the most famous posters from this period was written by an electrician and former Red Guard, Wei Jingsheng, who argued that Deng Xiaoping's campaign advocating the Four Modernizations (of agriculture, industry, technology, and national defense) should include a fifth modernization, democracy, without which the other four would be meaningless. The poster concludes with a strident call: "Xidan Democracy Wall has become the first battlefield in the people's fight against reactionaries. . . . Let us unite under this great and real banner and march toward modernization for the sake of the people's peace, happiness, rights and freedom!"[2]

The Democracy Wall featured not only political statements but also cultural ones. The poet Huang Xiang, for instance, came to Beijing to post on the Xidan wall a poem he had originally composed six years earlier, during the Cultural Revolution. Entitled "Confessions of the Great Wall," the poem adopts the voice of the Wall and opens with a description of the structure seeing itself as a mere "crack" on the surface of the globe, as if from a bird's-eye or even an extraterrestrial perspective:

> The earth is small and blue
> I am nothing but a small crack in it.
>
> Under gray, low-flying clouds in the sky
> I have been standing here for a long time.
> My legs are numb, I am losing my balance.
> I am falling down and dying of old age.
> . . .
> I am old.
> My descendants hate me.
> They hate me the way one hates a stubborn old grandfather.
> When they see me they turn their faces.

The poem develops this vision of the Wall's having fallen into obscurity and physical neglect, concluding with a description of the structure's "death":

> My ramparts are disappearing from the surface of the earth,
> Collapsing within the minds of the entire human race.

I am leaving; I have already died.
A generation of sons and grandsons are carrying me into the
museum,
Placing me together with dinosaur fossils.
I will not leave anything behind in this world
I will take everything I brought with me.
In the earth I have inhabited,
Science and revolution, friendship and understanding are
like a crowd
Of honored guests
Who pass through the long, dark night of the soul
And together cross the threshold into the future.[3]

The irony is that Huang Xiang figuratively grants the Wall a voice just as the Wall is described as "cross[ing] the threshold into the future." The implication, in other words, is that it is the prospect of demolition and oblivion that has helped grant the structure its new life and voice as a symbolic entity.

In December 1979 the government decided that the Xidan demonstrations had gone far enough and officially shut down the Democracy Wall. While the immediate political success of the Xidan wall was perhaps rather limited, it did establish a precedent for public expression that included not only explicitly political messages, such as Wei Jingsheng's manifesto, but also artistic and cultural statements, such as Huang Xiang's Wall poem. More of these artistic possibilities were developed the following September, when an experimental art group known as the Stars was denied permission to exhibit in Beijing's National Gallery and decided instead to display its members' works informally in the public space just outside the gallery. When the ad hoc exhibit was shut down by the police the next day, the group responded by organizing—on October first, the thirtieth anniversary of the founding of the PRC—a march from the Xidan Democracy Wall to the headquarters of the Beijing

Municipal Party Committee, carrying a banner that read, "We demand democracy and artistic freedom."

The short-lived 1979 Stars exhibit is regarded as having helped usher in the increasingly vibrant experimental art scene that arose in the 1980s. Initially, this avant-garde movement consisted primarily of graphic and installation pieces, but by the middle of the decade it began to include performance works as well. In 1986, for instance, Concept 21st Century realized its second performance, at the Gubeikou section of the Wall outside Beijing. The performance was entitled simply *Concept 21: The Great Wall,* and featured as its motto Mao's line, "If you haven't been to the Great Wall, you are not a real man."[4] A dozen or so artists dressed in red and black, with strips of white cloth wrapped around their head and body, proceeded to perform a series of ritualistic gestures and choreographed dance movements. The act of wrapping the body in white bandages was a recurrent theme in performance art in China in the 1980s, connoting among other things an image of bodily wounds or scars. (One of the literary movements to emerge in the late 1970s and early 1980s, known as "scar literature," focused in vivid and often quasi-autobiographical terms on the physical and psychological "scars" suffered during the Cultural Revolution.) Collectively, these alienating—and alienated—works posed the question of what it means to be a "real man"—which is to say, to be human—in contemporary China.

The wave of oppositional and experimental political-cultural expression sparked by the Xidan Democracy Wall and the Stars exhibit culminated a decade later, in 1989, with two major avant-garde art exhibits in January and February (one of which was explicitly presented as a commemoration of the tenth anniversary of the original Stars exhibit), followed by the pro-democracy Tiananmen Square protests that began in mid-May. The latter demonstrations, which were manifestly political, could also be seen as thoroughly cultural—as a sort of collective exercise in public performance. The military crackdown at Tiananmen Square on the morning of June 4 not only constituted a considerable setback for critical political discourse in China but also placed a significant damper on experimental artistic expression, which had flourished in the 1980s.

Just as the cultural implications of the Democracy Wall movement were dramatized by Huang Xiang's 1979 poem granting the Wall a figurative voice, the cultural ramifications of the 1989 Tiananmen Square protests were similarly developed in a creative work that attempted to allow the Wall to "speak." In June 1990, during the first anniversary of the 1989 protests, the conceptual artist Xu Bing—who is best known for his *Book from the Sky* project (1987–1991), which consisted of a vast text composed from a lexicon of more than four thousand ideographs he invented by taking components of existing ideographs and rearranging them to form new, "false" ones—assembled a team of thirty students and laborers and took them to the Jinshanling section of the Wall north of Beijing, where they spent twenty-four days balanced on rickety scaffolding while pounding the Wall with ink pads and paper.[5]

Xu Bing dressed himself and his team in uniforms decorated with the "pseudo-graphs" from his *Book from the Sky* project, and they employed a technique traditionally used to trace inscriptions from stone stelae to "translate" the Wall's markings into virtual text. Like the pseudo-graphs in *Book from the Sky*, the tracings of the Wall's surface could be seen as a mirror image of conventional writing, visually resembling textual inscription yet lacking any semantic content. Xu Bing's Wall rubbings in effect constituted a sort of wordless scripture—a text whose meaning is not contained within itself but rather is projected onto it by its viewers.

As Xu Bing and his crew were pounding out these ink rubbings of the surface of the Wall, the office of China's minister of culture published an essay attacking the contemporary avant-garde art scene. The essay, which appeared on the anniversary of the June Fourth

Ghosts Pounding on the Wall, Xu Bing (1990).
Courtesy of Xu Bing Studio.

crackdown on the Tiananmen Square demonstrators, singled out *Book from the Sky* for critique and likened it to a ghostly wall that entraps travelers as they run in circles trying frantically to escape. The folk saying cited in the article, *gui da qiang*, is used here in the sense of "ghosts building a wall" but could also be translated more literally to mean "ghosts *beating* a wall." This, of course, described perfectly the process by which Xu Bing and his team were quite literally pounding the surface of the Wall with ink pads and paper, and so Xu Bing decided to take the wording of this phrase that had been used against him and reappropriate it as the title for his new project—thereby implicitly putting his crew in the position of virtual ghosts simultaneously "pounding" the Wall and "building" a textual replica of the structure.

When Xu Bing first exhibited *Ghosts Pounding on the Wall* in 1991, after immigrating to America, he taped the thousands of sheets of rubbings together to create a thirty-two-meter by fifteen-meter replica of the Wall. More than a strict representation of the Wall, *Ghosts Pounding the Wall* translates the physical structure into text. Just as *Book from the Sky* attempted to desacralize the Chinese written language by de-linking its semantic dimension from its institutional context, *Ghosts* challenges the Wall's symbolic power by shifting attention from the monument's status as a material entity to the symbolic network within which it is embedded. *Ghosts,* in other words, presents the Wall as an entity with no inherent meaning of its own—a wordless scripture that derives its significance from the vision and aspirations projected onto it. The artistic significance of Xu Bing's *Ghosts* lies not merely in the actual installations in which the Wall rubbings are exhibited to the public but, equally importantly, in the transformative *process* by which the work was created in the first place (as seen in the video recording Xu Bing made of the painstaking labor that produced the work).

A similar theme of corporeality and transformation was picked up a few years later by a group of young artists living in a rundown neighborhood on the outskirts of the capital that they nicknamed Beijing's East Village. Many of the artists were trained as painters, but around 1993 several of them began pursuing an interest in performance, in which they would frequently use little more than their own body to comment on their position at the margins of various social and political orthodoxies. One member of this group, Ma Liuming, who had a slight physique and delicate features, became known for a series of performances in which he would use the contrast between his naked male body and his effeminate long hair and made-up face to create a sexually indeterminate alter ego that he dubbed "Fen/Ma Liuming." Ma developed variations on this conceit for nearly a decade, and in one 1998 performance he used the

Fen/Ma Liuming Walking along the Wall, Ma Liuming (1998).
Courtesy of Ma Liuming.

Simatai section of the Wall as a backdrop—creating a stark contrast between the soft vulnerability of his naked flesh and the solid stone surface of the Wall beneath his feet.[6]

Ma Liuming's Simatai performance could be seen as underscoring a contrast between the artist's transgendered performance and the legendary solidity of the Wall, or it could be understood as presenting a *parallel* between the artist's gender transformation and the Wall's own phoenix-like cycle of destruction and rebirth. Alternatively, it could even be interpreted as a metacommentary on these underlying issues of continuity and rupture as they relate to the relationship between performance and representation—asking, in effect, what it means to preserve (and own) a stable image of an inherently transient performance.

Actually, the Simatai performance was positioned at a critical fork in Ma's artistic trajectory, as it took place on the eve of two parallel developments in his attitude toward his own work. In 1998 he began a series of interactive performances in which he would appear naked onstage, as his Fen/Ma Liuming performative alter ego, and allow members of the audience to come up and pose with him as they wished. That same year, Ma and other East Village artists stopped collaborating with photographers Rong Rong and Xing Danwen (whose images of their performances had been critical to helping several of them achieve fame in the first place), because of a bitter dispute over who owned the rights to the photographs of their performances. Thus, in the period following his Simatai performance, Ma Liuming was surrendering partial control over his performances to his audience while simultaneously struggling to *regain* control over the photographs taken of his earlier works. By a similar logic, Ma's Simatai performance—one of his only works set against a recognizable landmark—could be seen as simultaneously laying claim to the image of the Wall while allowing the monument to partially usurp his position as the focal point of his own work.

The dispute between the performance artists and the photographers reflects not only abstract concerns with issues of intellectual property but also very concrete considerations of commodity value. Indeed, during the 1990s the worth of many of these artworks exploded, influencing the artists' relationship with their work and also becoming an explicit theme of some of the works themselves. Artists such as Wang Qiang, Xu Yihui, and Liu Zhang, for instance, explored issues of artistic commodification by printing images of Chinese and foreign currency on surfaces ranging from canvases to ceramics to plastic beads. The Guangzhou-based artist Lin Yilin constructed a series of walls out of bricks and paper money, and then placed himself inside the body-shaped openings he had left in them—thereby creating the appearance that he was embedded within his own work.[7] The resulting image of a human figure trapped inside a brick wall resonates with the legends of corvée workers buried within the Wall, while alluding to our own position within a figurative wall of monetary and commodity relations.

The Result of 1,000 Pieces, Lin Yilin (1994). Courtesy of Lin Yilin.

Another elegant commentary on China's ambivalent attitude toward global capital can be found in a series of performances by Beijing-based artist Wang Jin. For one work, Wang took bricks from the outer wall of Beijing's Forbidden City, printed them with images of U.S. hundred-dollar bills, and then returned the bricks to the dilapidated wall from which they had come. Wang Jin's "cash bricks" dramatized the tension between China's enthusiastic embrace of foreign investment and foreign trade, on one hand, and the nation's concurrent attempts to erect a virtual wall around its domestic economy, on the other. Wang Jin entitled his performance *Knocking at the Door*—alluding to the long-term economic consequences of Deng Xiaoping's Open Door policy, and also to the perception that foreign capital was knocking on the figurative door of China's (still partially closed) domestic economy.[8]

In 2001, the German artist H. A. Schult lined up 1,000 life-size statues in two parallel rows along a three-kilometer stretch of the same Jinshanling section of the Wall that Xu Bing had used for his

Ghosts Pounding the Wall.[9] Schult had begun this project five years earlier, when he and a team of thirty assistants spent six months creating a virtual army of colorful humanoid figures out of crushed cans, computer components, discarded plastic and cardboard, and other detritus. Schult's objective was to underscore our relationship to the mountain of waste we throw away every day, and he described his statues as "silent witnesses to a consumer age that has created an ecological imbalance worldwide." Borrowing a biblical ashes-to-ashes metaphor to describe his vision of contemporary human existence, he elaborates: "We produce garbage and we will be garbage. I created one thousand sculptures of garbage. They are a mirror of ourselves." Schult first exhibited the sculptures at the Xanten amphitheater in Germany in 1996 and then transported them to various sites around the world, including La Défense in Paris, Moscow's Red Square, the Egyptian pyramids, New York City, and finally Antarctica in 2008. It was at Jinshanling, however, that Schult's humanoid statues found their most powerful setting, resonating with the army of life-size terra-cotta warriors that the First Emperor had constructed to defend his tomb after his death, and with the army of laborers he is reputed to have buried beneath the Wall that he built to defend his empire while he was still alive.

Schult's 2001 *Trash People at the Great Wall,* meanwhile, was transformed at the precise moment of its inception when a local artist by the name of He Chengyao insinuated herself into the grand opening of the exhibit. As Schult was walking between the parallel rows of statues, flanked by photographers and a coterie of guests, He Chengyao spontaneously removed the red shirt she was wearing and proceeded to march, topless, between the rows in front of him—an act of artistic intercession that was captured by the same photographers who were there to document the exhibit's opening ceremony.[10] While He Chengyao's topless performance may have resembled the use of nudity in performances by Ma Liuming and his East Village colleagues in the 1990s, in He Chengyao's case it

Opening Up the Wall,
He Chengyao (2001).
Courtesy of He Chengyao.

turned out that the act had a more personal significance. The artist's
mother had given birth to her out of wedlock while still a teenager,
and the resulting public condemnation had taken such a toll on her
mother that she suffered a nervous breakdown that led her to pa-
rade naked through the streets of her hometown. He Chengyao's
2001 nude Wall performance, therefore, could be seen as an attempt to symbolically reaffirm her mother's dignity while also figuratively "reclaiming" the Wall from an act of foreign artistic appropriation.

In addition to its personal significance for the artist, He Chengyao's performance also speaks more generally to the politics of the Wall itself, as well as to China's contemporary efforts to reassert symbolic control over its own national landmark. Borrowing the same term Deng Xiaoping had used for his Reform and Opening-Up Campaign, He Chengyao entitled her impromptu performance at Simatai *Opening Up the Wall*—alluding to her attempt to figuratively "open up" not only Schult's Simatai installation but also the general significance of the Wall. Indeed, this title could be applied to virtually all of the avant-garde Wall performances, insofar as they all seek to push the structure beyond its current meaning and "open it up" to new possibilities.

This theme of opening up the Wall aptly describes, for instance, Cai Guo-Qiang's 1993 work *Project to Extend the Great Wall by 10,000 Meters: Project for Extraterrestrials No. 10,* which sought to "extend" our understanding of the Wall by literally exploding it. Three years later a similar sentiment was developed in two of Wang Jin's works. The first, *The Great Wall: To Be or Not to* Be, was to have been set near the same Jiayuguan section of the Wall where Cai Guo-Qiang had performed his *Extend the Great Wall,* though in place of Cai's explosives Wang Jin planned to create his virtual extension of the Wall out of a line of mud-filled Coca-Cola bottles and cans. Wang's second work from that year, *Ice Wall: '96 Central China,* was commissioned by the Zhengzhou municipal government to commemorate the opening of the city's first major shopping mall, and was conceived as a thirty-meter-long wall built out of 600 large blocks of ice embedded with consumer goods, ranging from cell phones to cameras and televisions to gold rings and bottles of perfume.[11] Both works were to have melded walls with modern commodities in a way that commented on the Wall's own process of commodification—wherein traditional views of the Wall are figuratively torn down and replaced by a contemporary vision of the Wall as a global commodity.

In the end neither of Wang Jin's 1996 works turned out exactly as planned. The *To Be or Not to Be* project eventually proved *not* to be and was never completed. The *Ice Wall* piece, meanwhile, was completed, but as soon as it was unveiled, it was swarmed by spectators intent on retrieving the valuable commodities buried inside. While the work was originally intended as an affirmation of the crystallized purity of the commodity form, its significance ultimately lay in its elicitation of a violent expression of desire that resulted in its own destruction. Both works, in other words, were ultimately realized as performances—with one functioning as a performance of destruction, and the other—paradoxically—as a performance of nonrealization.

Like Wang Jin's earlier *Knocking at the Door* performance, the *Ice Wall* project did not, of course, feature *the* Wall, though it did bring together several of the themes that underlie contemporary understandings of the Wall. The consumer goods embedded within the ice blocks constituted the precise inverse of the bodies of the workers traditionally imagined to have been buried beneath the Wall, just as the spectators' destruction of the wall mirrored Lady Meng Jiang's demolishment of the Wall with her tears. Implicitly evoking a vision of the Wall as a ravenous consumer of Chinese labor, Wang Jin's ice wall contained embedded within itself the consumer commodities that, according to orthodox Marxist theory, are the crystallized products of the labor process. Like the thirty-two-meter ink rubbing of the Wall that Xu Bing produced, Wang Jin's thirty-meter ice wall could be seen as an inverse reflection of the Wall—a commentary on the tension between labor and processes of commodification that have helped yield the Wall as we know it today.

Henan Province—the site of Wang Jin's *Ice Wall*—is sometimes referred to as Zhongyuan, or "central plains," in recognition of its position in the heart of China's Central Plains region, and it was here that the Shang dynasty oracle bones were initially unearthed at the end of the nineteenth century. This is also the region where, in

2002, a long stretch of stone wall was discovered that—it was claimed—dated back to the Warring Kingdoms state of Chu. This would have made it China's oldest surviving "long wall," though other researchers pointed out that no corroborating historical or archaeological evidence has been found to support the pre-Qin date—suggesting, in effect, that the structure's alleged antiquity was likely a mirage, an illusory reflection of the Wall whose future construction it was anticipating.

The flurry of excitement around this apparent discovery of an early long wall happened to coincide with the unveiling of a more significant "secret" hidden at the very heart of this heartland region. In 2001, Beijing acknowledged for the first time that tainted blood in the nation's blood supply accounted for a "significant percentage" of the HIV epidemic that had plagued rural Henan for much of the preceding decade. The figurative unveiling, in Henan Province, of Wang Jin's *Ice Wall* in 1996 and of the Chu state wall six years later both took place against the backdrop of a domestic AIDS epidemic centered in rural Henan, the severity of which was neither acknowledged nor well understood.

While the details of China's domestic AIDS crisis did not begin to come to light until the late 1990s, as early as 1988 Beijing had begun to implement a national quarantine system that came to be known as a "Great Wall against AIDS." By adopting a strategy of testing foreigners entering China and rejecting foreign blood products, the government's AIDS Wall reinforced the belief that the virus was an external threat that could be stopped at the border. In practice, however, a primary consequence of the policy was a quarantine on useful information about the domestic epidemic, which exacerbated the crisis by hampering the possibility of an effective response. The result was a paradox wherein the AIDS Wall was transformed from its intended purpose of protecting the nation from the crisis to actually facilitating the crisis (just as the HIV virus itself functions by transforming the human immune system from a barrier against infection into a portal for the virus's entry).

Beijing's belated acknowledgment in 2001 of the circumstances and severity of China's domestic AIDS epidemic roughly coincided with a more general unraveling of the government's ability to control the dissemination of information within its own borders. From the deadly 2001 explosion of a Jiangxi school building that was secretly being used to manufacture fireworks to the 2002 deaths of customers who ate poison-laced food from a Jiangsu breakfast stall, there have been a number of high-profile tragedies in China that the government initially attempted to keep under wraps but were subsequently brought to light after a wave of disclosures and exposés posted on the Internet.

Over the past decade the Internet has emerged as one of the key elements in China's attempt to modernize and internationalize its economy, while at the same time becoming one of the most visible challenges to China's efforts to control the movement of information within its borders. Beijing has responded to the threat by developing what is known within China as the Golden Shield Project and abroad as the Great Firewall of China. This virtual firewall has been designed to restrict access to certain news sites and sites with user-generated content, and also to screen e-mails and messages for a set of banned terms. In practice, however, the firewall has proven to be rather porous, as it not only allows a significant percentage of the banned terms to get through but also encourages Internet users to resort to using coded language or technical workarounds to sidestep the restrictions—a practice known in Chinese as *fanqiang*, or "climbing the wall."

In 2009 the government announced that all new computers sold in China would come with a preinstalled software package known as Green Dam, which was ostensibly designed to prevent youths from accessing porn sites but which was revealed to also block access to politically sensitive sites. This new policy was widely criticized in China and abroad and was ultimately rescinded. The matter resurfaced six months later, however, when a Michigan-based company specializing in parental-control Web filters announced it was suing the Chinese government and other parties for stealing its software for the Green Dam program. If the allegation is true, it would mean that the latest incarnation of the Great Firewall (like the modern vision of the Wall as a national icon) was literally a foreign import.

One example of the paradoxical significance of the Internet and the Great Firewall in China can be found in Premier Wen Jiabao's Facebook "wall." Appointed premier of the State Council in 2003, Wen Jiabao came to be known as the "people's premier" because of his efforts to make the government more accessible and accountable. Shortly after his appointment, Wen helped push for a more active response to the unfolding SARS epidemic, and nine months later he became the first high-level official to address the nation's HIV/AIDS epidemic. In 2006 he issued a State Council decree enforcing the Regulations on the Protection of the Wall. When an earthquake devastated Sichuan in May 2008, Wen (who is a geologist by training) traveled to the region just hours after the quake. Shortly after the calamity, a Facebook page appeared under Wen's name that quickly attracted an outpouring of support for his response to the quake, and by the end of the year the page had acquired more than seventy thousand "fans" and more than ten thousand messages had been posted to his "wall"—the publically accessible portion of a Facebook page on which visitors can leave messages, much as tourists leave graffiti on the surface of the Wall itself.

Just as Kafka argued that an emperor's power is a product of the vast gulf that inevitably intervenes between him and his subjects, Wen Jiabao's popularity comes not despite but rather *because of* the vast distance that separates the people's premier from his people.

The premier's Facebook page, while appearing to reinforce Wen's reputation for accessibility, is actually symptomatic of the gap that exists between him and the citizens he represents. The popularity of the page continued to grow after Facebook began to be blocked intermittently in China a month or so before the 2008 Olympics. Even after access to Facebook in China was cut off entirely a year later, Wen's page remains a site of animated (and presumably expatriate and international) dialogue about Chinese governmental policies and other matters.

Both the Great Firewall and the AIDS Wall capture a critical paradox that defines the contemporary Wall itself. The so-called Great Firewall of China, for instance, symbolizes China's attempts to protect itself from the destabilizing effects of the Web while underscoring the Web's status as a link between China and the same outside world from which it is trying to protect itself. China's Great Wall against AIDS, similarly, represents the nation's attempt to insulate itself from the global HIV/AIDS pandemic, even as, in practice, it inadvertently helped facilitate the progress of China's domestic epidemic. More generally, the Wall itself has traditionally functioned—and continues to function—not so much as an absolute barrier between China and the world, but as a bridge facilitating the introduction and incorporation of external elements into the national body (politic).

Return to Origins

When he thought of there being so many hymens throughout the country, lined up like a Great Wall of troops waiting for him, Baldy Li couldn't help excitedly scratching his thighs with both hands.

—Yu Hua, *Brothers* (2006)

A song by the military composer Meng Qingyun poses what a recent *People's Daily* article describes as a "five-hundred-year-old-question": Just how long *is* the Wall? The song begins,

Everyone says that our homeland lies on both sides of the
Long Wall
Do *you* know how long the Long Wall is?
One end leaps over the cold moon in the desert mountain pass
While the other end stretches into the hearts of the children
of Hua and Xia.[1]

Even as this piece appears to reinforce a conventional view of China's most famous landmark as a national icon, in practice its opening lines translate the Wall's significance from a geographical plane ("one end leaps over the cold moon in the desert mountain pass") to a cultural one ("the other end stretches into the hearts of the children of Hua and Xia"). The reference to the children of the Hua and Xia—the legendary ancestors of the Chinese race—alludes simultaneously to China's past as well as its future, suggesting that the Wall may be seen as a figurative blank screen onto which the nation's collective dreams and aspirations may be projected.

While this children's song emphasizes the Wall's cultural and psychological dimensions, the structure's military connotations make a mediated return in the form of the song's suggestion, further on, that if we want to know where the Wall lies, we need only look for the "endless row of bodies dressed in green uniforms." This reference to a row of uniform-clad "bodies" functions as a reminder of the Wall's military connotations, and also recalls the image of the Wall as concealing an endless row of bodies of the corvée laborers and soldiers ostensibly buried beneath it. We find a similar formulation of the Wall's corporeal and military underpinnings in a recent work by Beijing-based author Yu Hua. Originally published in two volumes in 2005 and 2006, the controversial best-selling novel *Brothers* traces China's transformation over the past four decades from Maoist orthodoxy to capitalist excess, culminating in a "national virgin beauty pageant" that was inspired by the protagonist Baldy Li's surreal vision of an endless row of all of the nation's hymens "lined up like a Great Wall of troops."

In Yu Hua's novel, this vision of a Wall of hymens has its origins in a sequence of events that can be traced back to Baldy Li's decision a decade earlier to have a vasectomy after discovering that the town beauty, with whom he had been infatuated ever since he was a boy, had rejected him in favor of his stepbrother. From this point on, Baldy Li's life is a rollercoaster ride that takes him from stable sinecure to abject poverty to obscene wealth. Under Deng Xiaoping's economic reform, he quits his state-guaranteed "iron rice-bowl" job at a local charity factory for handicapped workers in order to start his own business, but fails spectacularly and ends up staging a one-man sit-in outside the local government building in an attempt to get his old job back. Having nothing better to do as he sits there day after day, he begins collecting empty bottles and old newspapers discarded by passersby, and from these humble beginnings he becomes filthy rich by developing a vast, nationwide recycling conglomerate. Baldy Li's resulting wealth brings him a host of problems, including a gaggle of women who file a collective paternity suit against him, but he brings the resulting trial to an uproarious halt when he presents the judge with a decade-old medical record of his vasectomy. He concludes by offering the court an emotional apology in which he confesses that, while it is true that he has slept with countless women, he nevertheless has never had the opportunity to experience "true love"—a romantic ideal that he conflates metonymically with an intact hymen. After melodramatic accounts of Baldy Li's desire for true love are published in newspapers throughout China, he finds himself swamped by letters from beautiful virgins offering their love—and it is precisely this outpouring of epistolary devotion from virtual (and ostensibly virginal) strangers that inspires his surreal vision of hymens lined up like troops.

Obsessed with this vision of a Great Wall of hymens, Baldy Li decides to make his fantasy of true love a reality by hosting what he describes as China's first National Hymen Olympic Competition. Yu Hua originally conceived the idea for this virgin beauty pageant at a time when "pageant fever" was sweeping the nation. After having been banned in China since the founding of the PRC, beauty pageants returned with a vengeance at the turn of the twenty-first century. In 2003, for instance, China's Hainan Island held a national Miss China pageant as a prelude to hosting the first Miss World competition in China. Over the next few years, China hosted a variety of other regional, national, and international beauty contests, including a Tourism Queen International pageant, a Top Model of the World competition, a "Zhen'ao National Contest of the Beauty of the Gray-Headed Group" for contestants over fifty-five, and three out of the next four Miss World competitions. Thus, during the first years of the new millennium, China's attempts to "march into the world" were often played out in a march down the catwalk, as the desire for national strength and recognition was increasingly sublimated into romantic and even sexual desire.

One of China's more peculiar variants on the beauty pageant tradition was the inaugural Miss Artificial Beauty pageant for plastic surgery recipients, held in December 2004. Inspired by a contestant who had been disqualified from a traditional pageant on the grounds that her beauty had been artificially enhanced, this pageant has quickly taken hold in a society that has embraced cosmetic surgery with a passion, spending more than $2.5 billion a year on cosmetic procedures. This craze has been driven in part by a fascination with the possibility of self-reinvention, the implications of which Yu Hua develops most dramatically in his description of Baldy Li's National Hymen Olympic Competition. Attracting more than three thousand contestants from around the country, the virgin competition appears at first blush to be a smashing success. We subsequently learn, however, that the pageant's beauty is only skin deep, and that the entire celebration is actually predicated on a sham. Few if any of the contestants are real virgins; instead they use a variety of techniques, ranging from hymen reconstruction surgery to artificial hymen inserts, to create the *illusion* of virginity.

Baldy Li's virgin beauty pageant culminates in a hilarious scene featuring a domestic brand of artificial hymen named after the legendary Lady Meng Jiang—ironically so, given that the name connotes not only a vision of the Wall as an impermeable barrier, but also the woman whose tears were responsible for the Wall's *collapse*. A Lady Meng Jiang hymen malfunctions at a critical moment on the eve of the pageant, exposing the underlying hypocrisy of the event as a whole. Just as the cultural significance of the hymen lies in the necessary possibility of its rupture, the symbolism of the Wall lies in its status not so much as an impregnable barrier, but as one that is necessarily vulnerable to being breached.

Yu Hua's satirical depiction of the duplicity of the fictional Na-

tional Hymen Olympics uncannily anticipated some of the most notorious scandals of the Beijing Olympics themselves—including al-
legations of lip-synching performers, ethnic impersonation, and age
falsification—together with the Olympics-inspired delay in revealing that several Chinese companies had been using deadly mela-
mine to mimic the presence of protein in infant formula. More generally, the Beijing Games could be seen as an elaborate facade, in
which China attempted to assume an "artificial hymen" of political
purity for the sake of its ongoing march into the world.

Yu Hua's positioning of the symbolic Wall at the intersection of
the twin ideals of love and illusion was also mirrored by an unrelated misadventure that took place in early 2006. In a harebrained
entrepreneurial scheme of which Baldy Li would have been proud,
a Chinese company—on Valentine's Day, no less—installed a replica of a section of the Wall near Badaling. Responding to the grow-
ing problem of graffiti on the Wall, this so-called Great Wall of
Love was presented as an opportunity for couples to inscribe oaths
of love and devotion on a Wall-like surface without having to de-
face the actual structure. With 9,999 bricks available for inscription
at a price of 999 yuan (approximately 123 U.S. dollars) a brick, the
Great Wall of Love theoretically could have netted the company
more than a million dollars. In the end, however, only four couples
purchased the figurative "cash bricks" before the project was shut
down on the grounds that the fake Wall was in "violation of cultural heritage protection regulations."

The charge that the Great Wall of Love went against cultural heritage regulations was not entirely unanticipated, and in fact the
project's organizers had from the very beginning attempted to pre-
empt this critique by clothing the project in a rhetoric of historical
preservation. They had specified, for instance, that a portion of the
proceeds would be donated to support the restoration of the actual
monument, and that the very presence of the Wall of Love would
help protect the *real* Wall from further desecration by providing

tourists with an acceptable surface on which to express themselves. In theory, therefore, the tourist site would help secure the integrity of the Great Wall, just as the Wall itself was conceived as a defensive structure to help protect the nation as a whole.

The name of the 2006 Badaling graffiti wall not only echoed Deng Xiaoping's earlier call to "*love* our country and restore the Great Wall" but also anticipated William Lindesay's coinage—for a Badaling cleanup project he organized later that same year—of the Mao-inspired motto, "If you don't *love* the Wall, you are not a real man." Lindesay used an emphasis on love and desire ("if you don't love the Wall") to articulate a version of Baldy Li's libidinal fantasy, that it was only through *loving* a Great Wall of hymens that he would be able to reassert his manhood. Lending unexpectedly literal connotations to the conventional English translation of Mao's dictum that it is only through a visit to the Wall that one can become a "true man," these contemporary examples present the Wall as a symbol of strength and male virility, but also as a perpetual reminder of a potentially emasculating challenge. The Great Wall of Love was explicitly presented as a *fake* Wall—a blank surface onto which tourists could literally inscribe their fantasies and desires. Yet perhaps the reason the project had to be shut down almost immediately after it opened was because it inadvertently came too close to the "truth" of the Wall. The Wall, in other words, is always already a "fake" Wall—a figurative screen onto which viewers may project an array of disparate values and ideals. It is, however, precisely this quality of being a "wordless scripture" in which viewers can inscribe their dreams and desires—as they were briefly able to do in a very literal sense with the Great Wall of Love—that has helped grant the structure its historical resilience.

In this volume, we have surveyed the Wall's history while examining its status within the contemporary imagination. I have attempted to challenge many of our conventional *assumptions* about the Wall's status as a monolithic and unitary entity, but only in order to redeem a set of underlying *intuitions* about the Wall's coherent identity. More specifically, I propose that the significance of this paradigmatic symbol of Chinese history, national borders, and physical enormity is ultimately determined by its position at the interstices of past and present, materiality and abstraction, China and the world. The virtually simultaneous unveilings of the Great Wall of Love tourist site and Yu Hua's fantasy of a Great Wall of hymens, meanwhile, underscores the fundamentally ephemeral nature of the Wall—suggesting that the "reality" of the modern Wall may be found in its status as a projection of society's collective fantasies and desires. The long-term stability of the Wall's identity lies not so much in any intrinsic continuity of appearance, purpose, or function of the structure, but in its status as a blank surface onto which viewers may project their dreams and aspirations. It is in the Wall's ephemeral and fractured nature, therefore, that we find the secret of the structure's status as a historically continuous and conceptually coherent entity.

Getting There

The vast majority of the extant Wall was built during the Ming dynasty, and many of the popular tourist sites have been extensively repaired during the past half century. These sites stretch from the Gulf of Bohai to the Ordos Desert, with the most popular ones clustered around Beijing. Below are brief introductions to the best-known of Wall sites.

Hebei Province: Shanhaiguan

The section of the Wall that is conventionally regarded as its easternmost terminus is located at Shanhaiguan in Hebei Province. Shanhaiguan, which means "mountain-sea pass," is the name of a historic town approximately fifteen kilometers northeast of the metropolitan center of the port city Qinhuangdao, and marks the point where the Wall reaches the sea. The site at which the Wall actually meets the Bohai Sea is known as Laolongtou (Old Dragon's Head). An important feature of Shanhaiguan is the Zhendong Tower, also known as "First Pass under Heaven," and other tourist attractions in the area include a Mengjiangnü Temple and a Great Wall museum.

Beijing Region

Many of the most popular sections of the Wall are located in the region around Beijing. Their location near the capital makes them easily accessible for tourists today, and it also means these sites were much more strategically important when the Wall was being constructed during the Ming.

Badaling and Juyongguan

Constructed mostly during the sixteenth century, Badaling has been the premier tourist section of the Wall ever since the poet-turned-bureaucrat Guo Moruo called for this stretch to be thoroughly repaired, in 1952. In 2001 the completion of the Badaling Expressway from the capital made traveling to this section of the Wall even more convenient. Actually, there are three separate Wall exits from the expressway. The first leads to Juyongguan Pass, which includes a fort and a stretch of the Wall. The next exit leads to a less-visited section, which features a steep section that affords climbers a spectacular view of the region, including part of the unrenovated "wild wall." Finally, the granddaddy of Wall tourist destinations, the Badaling section, is accessible from the third Wall exit on the expressway. Accoutered with amenities ranging from a cable car and a Starbucks to a pit of black bears, Badaling is visited by millions of people every year.

Mutianyu

Located east of Juyongguan, Mutianyu is one of the best-preserved sections of the Wall and is easily accessible from Beijing by bus, train, or car. Construction at Mutianyu began in the early Ming, on a site where the Northern Qi had previously erected walls during the sixth century. Designed to protect the capital as well as the

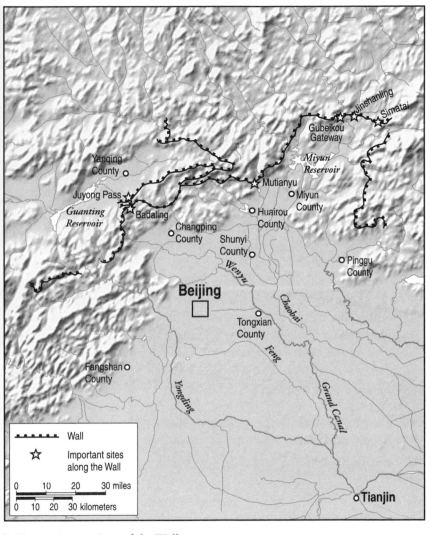

Beijing-region sections of the Wall.

Meridian Mapping.

imperial tombs, this section features twenty-two densely arranged watchtowers, and is unusual in that it features crenellations on both sides of the wall, permitting it to be defended against attacks from either direction.

Gubeikou, Jinshanling, and Simatai

East of Mutianyu are the Gubeikou Pass and the adjoining Jinshanling and Simatai sections of the structure. Located about 130 kilometers from Beijing and accessible by train, tour bus, or taxi, Gubeikou is the site of a critical pass through the Yanshan Mountains. To the east of the pass is the 10-kilometer-long Jinshanling section of the Wall. The initial section at Jinshanling has been extensively repaired, but the Wall becomes progressively more dilapidated as one approaches Simatai. Still, it is possible to hike directly from Jinshanling to Simatai, a distance of about 30 kilometers. The approximately 5-kilometer-long section of the Wall at Simatai is regarded as one of the most impressive. Precipitously steep in many places, this portion of the structure has undergone comparatively little repair in the modern period (compared with other major tourist sections of the Wall), and consequently the original Ming surface is particularly evident (which is probably why Xu Bing chose this section in 1990 for taking ink impressions of the side of the structure in his *Ghosts Pounding the Wall* performance).

Gansu Province: Jiayuguan

Meaning "precious jade pass," Jiayuguan is the site of one of the westernmost sections of the Wall, and it features one of the largest passes and best-preserved Ming forts. The Wall is located about six kilometers from the city of Jiayuguan, from which tourists can take taxis out and back. Construction on the pass began as early as 1372. According to a well-known legend, the official overseeing the construction asked the foreman how many bricks would be needed. Upon being told the number, the official expressed concern that that wouldn't be enough, so the foreman added one more. When the pass was completed, precisely one brick was left over, and it is still on display today.

Further Reading

The following is a select and annotated list of works readers may wish to consult. Intended for general readers, this list includes only reasonably accessible English-language publications related to the topics discussed in each chapter.

Chapter 1

The first book written about the Wall was William Geil's 1909 volume, *The Great Wall of China* (New York: Sturgis and Walton Company, 1909). An amateur adventurer, Geil spent four months in 1908 trekking the entire length of the Wall. When he returned to the United States he published a richly illustrated 400-page monograph, which he said would be "so complete that the future historian of the Wall would find little to write about unless he pirated our notes."

Needless to say, "future historians" have hardly found themselves at a loss when it comes to writing about the Wall. One of the most influential modern books on the topic, for instance, is Arthur Waldron's *The Great Wall of China: From History to Myth* (Cambridge: Cambridge University Press, 1990), which argues that the popular notion of a unitary and historically continuous Great Wall is actually a modern myth. Waldron's thesis has been quite influential in Western writings about the Wall. Julia Lovell, for instance, in her recent book, *The Great Wall: China against the World 1000 BC–AD 2000* (New York: Grove Press, 2006), echoes Waldron in her opening claim that "the first great myth of the Great Wall is its singularity" and then proceeds to use the Wall as a lens through which to survey a 3,000-year history of "China against the world." The British photographer and distance runner William Lindesay has also published several books on the Wall, ranging from *Alone on the Great Wall from the Desert to the Sea* (London: Hodder and Stoughton, 1989), describing his initial trek along the Wall, to his grandiosely titled *The Great Wall: China's Historical Wonder and Mankind's Most Formidable Construction Project* (New York: Norton, 2002). More recently he has published a volume of photographs entitled *The Great Wall Revisited: From Jade Gate to Old Dragon's Head* (Cambridge, Mass.: Harvard University Press, 2008), in which Lindesay strategically juxtaposes a series of late-nineteenth and early twentieth-century photographs with recent "rephotographs" that he himself took of the same sites.

Chapter 2

The locus classicus of discussions of the Qin dynasty Wall is Sima Qian's historical Han dynasty text, the *Shiji*. There are several translations of this text, including Burton Watson's *Records of the Grand Historian,* in three volumes (New York: Columbia University Press, 1993). A detailed discussion of this period can be found in the first volume of the *Cambridge History of China* (Cambridge: Cambridge University Press, 1986), and volume three of Joseph Needham's monumental *Science and Civilisation in China* (Cambridge: Cambridge University Press, 1959) contains a well-documented survey of technologies of wall building in China, including those that were employed in constructing the original Qin Wall.

Chapter 3

A comprehensive overview of pre-Qin China can be found in *The Cambridge History of Ancient China* (Cambridge: Cambridge University Press, 1999), added as a prequel to the *Cambridge History of China* (which was conceived and begun before the recent explosion of archaeological discoveries transformed our understanding of the early pre-Qin period). In *Ancient China and Its Enemies: The Rise of Nomadic Power in East Asian History* (Cambridge: Cambridge University Press, 2002), Nicola di Cosmo presents a good examination of China's relationship with the various pastoral-nomadic groups along its periphery. Translations of several different versions of the Lady Meng Jiang legend can be found in Wilt Idema's *Meng Jiangnü Brings Down the Great Wall: Ten Versions of a Chinese Legend* (Seattle: University of Washington Press, 2008), and a useful overview of the Wang Zhaojun legend can be found in Uradyn Bulaq, *The Mongols at China's Edge: History and the Politics of National Identity* (Lanham, Md.: Rowman and Littlefield, 2002).

Chapter 4

A detailed discussion of the military campaign out of which the Ming dynasty Wall emerged may be found in Frederick W. Mote, "The T'u Mu Incident of 1449," in *Chinese Ways of Warfare,* ed. Frank Kierman, Jr., and John K. Fairbank (Cambridge, Mass.: Harvard University Press, 1974). Numerous editions of Marco Polo's *Travels* are available, but one of the most useful is the two-volume *The Travels of Marco Polo: The Complete Yule-Cordier Edition* (New York: Dover Publications, 1993). Critical treatment of Polo's text and his voyage can be found in John Larner, *Marco Polo and the Discovery of the World* (New Haven: Yale University Press, 1999), and an influential (and problematic) interrogation of the authenticity of Polo's narrative can be found in Frances Wood, *Did Marco Polo Go to China?* (Boulder, Colo.: Westview Press, 1996).

Chapter 5

A readable overview of the social and political developments of modern China can be found in Jonathan Spence's *In Search of Modern China* (New York: Norton, 1999). A more specific analysis of the discourses of conservatism and reform during the early twentieth-century period is offered in Yü-sheng Lin's classic study, *Crisis of Chinese Consciousness* (Madison: University of Wisconsin Press, 1978) and, more recently, in David Apter and Tony Saich's *Revolutionary Discourse in Mao's Republic* (Cambridge, Mass.: Harvard University Press, 1998).

Chapter 6

Two major exhibits on the Wall in 1996 yielded useful companion volumes about the Wall and the cultural production it has inspired. Claire Roberts and Geremie Barmé's edited volume *The Great Wall of China* (Sydney: Powerhouse Publishing, 2006) was prepared for a Wall exhibit organized jointly by museums in Sydney and Beijing, and Gao Minglu's *The Wall: Reshaping Contemporary Chinese Art* (Buffalo: Buffalo Fine Arts Academy, 2006) was prepared as the catalogue for a similar exhibit by organizations in Buffalo, New York, and Beijing. While the latter volume is somewhat difficult to obtain, a version of Gao's useful introduction was published separately under the title, "The Great Wall in Chinese Contemporary Art" in the journal *positions: east asian cultures critique* (Winter 2004). University of Chicago–based art historian and curator Wu Hung has also written several books on China's contemporary art scene that feature useful discussions of many of the artists discussed in this volume, including *Exhibiting Experimental Art in China* (Chicago: David and Alfred Smart Museum of Art, 2000) and *Transience: Chinese Experimental Art at the End of the Twentieth Century* (Chicago: University of Chicago Press, 2005).

Notes

Unless otherwise noted, all translations are my own.

Book epigraphs: *Xunzi,* book 5; for another translation, see *Xunzi: A Translation and Study of the Complete Works: Vol. 1, Books 1–6,* trans. John Knoblock (Stanford: Stanford University Press, 1988), 206. Jorge Luis Borges, "La muralla y los libros," in Borges, *Òbras Completas,* vol. 4 (Buenos Aires: Emecé, 2005), 13; for another translation, see Borges, "The Wall and the Books," in *Other Inquisitions, 1937–1952,* trans. Ruth L. C. Simms (Austin: University of Texas Press, 1975), 5. Michel de Certeau, *The Practice of Everyday Life,* trans. Stephen Rendall (Berkeley: University of California Press, 1984), 171, reprinted courtesy of University of California Press.

Prologue

1. Charles Hutzler, "A Great Wall: Obama Tours China's Iconic Site," Associated Press, November 18, 2009.
2. William Edgar Geil, *The Great Wall of China* (New York: Sturgis and Walton Company, 1909), 8.
3. Video posted online at *Row 2 Seat 4: Fox News' White House View,* whitehouse.blogs.foxnews.com/?p=5708, November 18, 2009.
4. "Obama Visits the Wall, 'Inspired by Its Majesty,'" *People's Daily Online,* November 19, 2009, http://english.peopledaily.com.cn/90001/90776/90883/6817379.html.

1. A Unity of Gaps

Epigraph: Franz Kafka, "The Great Wall of China," in *Kafka's Selected Stories,* trans. and ed. Stanley Corngold (New York: W. W. Norton, 2007), 115; translation modified.

1. Immanuel Kant, *Critique of Judgment,* trans. John Bernard (New York: Cosimo Classics, 2007), 64.

2. John Barrow, *Travels in China, Containing Descriptions, Observations, and Comparisons, Made and Collected in the Course of a Short Residence at the Imperial Palace of Yuen-Min-Yuen, and on a Subsequent Journey through the Country from Pekin to Canton* (London: Cadell and W. Davies, 1804), 334.

3. Jing Ai, *Zhongguo chang cheng shi* [A history of China's Long Wall] (Shanghai: Renmin chubanshe, 2006), 340.

4. Cited in Paul Mooney, "Great Wall of China Overrun, Damaged, Disneyfied," in *National Geographic News,* May 15, 2007.

5. Neil Armstrong, interviewed by Stephen Ambrose and Douglas Brinkley, *NASA Johnson Space Center Oral History Project* (September 19, 2001), 86.

6. Ed Lu, quoted in Robert Britt, "What's Really Visible from Space," Space.com, www.space.com/scienceastronomy/visible_from_space_031006.html, October 6, 2003.

7. Quoted in Bob Considine, *Ripley: The Modern Marco Polo* (New York: Doubleday, 1961), 81.

8. Robert Ripley, "The Great Wall of China," *Believe It or Not!* (1932).

9. Joseph Needham, *Science and Civilisation in China,* vol. 3: *Mathematics and the Sciences of the Heavens and the Earth* (Cambridge: Cambridge University Press, 1959), 47.

10. William Stukeley et al., *The Family Memoirs of the Rev. William Stukeley* (Durham: Surtees Society, 1882–1887), vol. 3, 142.

11. Edward Gibbon, *The History of the Decline and Fall of the Roman Empire,* vol. 3 (London: Methuen and Company, 1901), 83.

12. Willard Van Orman Quine, *Word and Object* (Cambridge, Mass.: MIT Press, 1964).

13. Jorge Luis Borges, "The Analytical Language of John Wilkins," *Other Inquisitions, 1937–1952,* trans. Ruth L. C. Simms (Austin: Univer-

sity of Texas Press, 1975), 101–105. Michel Foucault, *The Order of Things: An Archeology of the Human Sciences* (New York: Routledge, 2002), xvi.

14. Arthur Waldron, *The Great Wall of China: From History to Myth* (Cambridge: Cambridge University Press, 1990), 27–28; emphasis added.
15. See Ron Mallon et al., "Semantics Cross-Cultural Style," *Cognition* 92 (2004): B1–B12.
16. Kafka, "The Great Wall of China," 113.
17. Ibid., 122–123.
18. "Plan to Raze Chinese Wall," reprinted in *Chicago Daily Tribune, June 26, 1899, cited and discussed in Museum of Hoaxes, www.museumofhoaxes.com/hoax/archive/permalink/the_*great_wall _of_china_hoax/.
19. Harry Lee Wilber, "A Fake That Rocked the World," *North American Review* 247, no. 1 (Spring 1939): 21–26.

2. Aspirations of Immortality

Epigraph: Sima Qian, *Shiji* [Records of the historian], chapter 6. Corresponding passage may be found in Sima Qian, *Records of the Grand Historian: Qin Dynasty*, trans. Burton Watson (New York: Columbia University Press, 1993), 43.

1. Sima Qian, *Shiji*, chapter 6; corresponding passage found in Sima Qian, *Records of the Grand Historian*, 53.
2. Sima Qian, *Shiji*, chapter 88, emphasis added; corresponding passage may be found in Sima Qian, *Records of the Grand Historian*, 207–208.
3. Derk Bodde, "The State and Empire of Ch'in," in Denis Twitchett, Michael Loewe, and John King Fairbank, *The Cambridge History of China*, vol. 1 (Cambridge: Cambridge University Press, 1986), 62. Jonathan Fryer, *The Great Wall of China* (London: New English Library, 1975), 50.
4. Translation adapted from Sima Qian, *Records of the Grand Historian*, 63.
5. Mao Zedong, "Speech at the Eighth National Congress of the Chinese Communist Party," May 8, 1958, cited in Li Yu-ning, *The First*

Emperor of China (New York: International Arts and Sciences Press, 1975), xlix–l.

6. Ibid.

7. *The Mummy: Tomb of the Dragon Emperor,* directed by Rob Cohen (Universal Pictures, 2008).

8. *Yingxiong* [Hero], directed by Zhang Yimou (Beijing New Picture Film, 2002).

9. Tan Dun, *The First Emperor,* Metropolitan Opera premiere, New York, 2006.

10. *Gujin dazhan Qin yong qing* [Fight and love with a terracotta warrior], directed by Ching Siu-tung (1990).

3. Between History and Legend

Epigraph: *Zhuangzi,* "Qiwu lun." Corresponding passage may be found in Zhuangzi, *Chuang Tzu: Basic Writings,* trans. Burton Watson (New York: Columbia University Press, 1996), 38.

1. Sima Qian, *Shiji,* chapter 110.

2. Ibid.; translation adapted from Arthur Waldron, *The Great Wall of China,* 17.

3. *Zhanguo ce* [Intrigues of the warring states], chapter 24; corresponding passage may be found in J. I. Crump, Jr., trans., *Chan-Kuo Ts'e* (Ann Arbor: Center for Chinese Studies, University of Michigan, 1996), 407.

4. Sima Qian, *Shiji,* chapter 6; corresponding passage may be found in Sima Qian, *Records of the Grand Historian,* 30; translation revised.

5. Sima Qian, *Shiji,* chapter 110.

6. Ban Gu, *Han shu* [Book of Han], chapter 94.

7. Uradyn Bulaq, *The Mongols at China's Edge: History and the Politics of National Identity* (Lanham, Md.: Rowman and Littlefield, 2002), 72.

8. Ban Gu, *Han shu,* chapter 94.

9. "Dao lianzi," cited in Yang Zhenliang, *Meng Jiangnü yanjiu* [Meng Jiangnü studies] (Taipei: Taiwan xueshen shuju, 1985). The first half of this translation is adapted from Wilt Idema, trans., *Meng Jiangnü Brings Down the Great Wall: Ten Versions of a Chinese Legend* (Seat-

tle: University of Washington Press, 2008), 11; the latter half of the translation is my own.

10. Cited in Idema, *Meng Jiangnü Brings Down the Great Wall,* 12–13.
11. *Zuozhuan,* "Xianggong, Year Twenty-three."
12. *Mengzi* [Mencius], chapter 6B; corresponding passage may be found in D. C. Lau, trans., *Mencius* (New York: Penguin Books, 1970), 175–176.
13. Liu Xiang, *Shuo yuan* [Garden of persuasions], chapter 11.
14. The text of the song first appears in Yang Quan's third-century text, *Wuli lun* [On the principle of things].
15. Translation from Sima Qian, *Records of the Grand Historian: Han Dynasty I,* trans. Burton Watson (New York: Columbia University Press, 1993), 242.

4. A Garden of Forking Paths

Epigraph: Jorge Luis Borges, "El jardín de los senderos que se bifurcan," in Borges, *Obras Completas,* vol. 4 (Buenos Aires: Emecé, 1989), 472–480. For another translation, see Jorge Luis Borges, "The Garden of Forking Paths," in *Jorge Luis Borges: Collected Fictions,* trans. Andrew Hurley (New York: Penguin Books, 1999), 125.

1. *Longmen kezhan* [Dragon Gate Inn], directed by King Hu (Union Film Company, 1967).
2. Eugene O'Neill and Travis Bogard, *The Unknown O'Neill: Unpublished or Unfamiliar Writings of Eugene O'Neill* (New Haven: Yale University Press, 1988), 229.
3. Thomas Astley, *A New Collection of Voyages and Travels,* compiled by John Green (London, 1745).
4. George Staunton, cited in Henry Yule, ed., *Book of Ser Marco Polo, the Venetian: Concerning the Kingdoms and Marvels of the East* (London: John Murray, 1871), 292.
5. Frances Wood, *Did Marco Polo Go to China?* (Boulder, Colo.: Westview Press, 1998).
6. Gaspar da Cruz, "A Treatise of China and the adjoyning Regions [. . .]," in Samuel Purchas, *Hakluytus Posthumus or Purchas His Pilgrimes* (Glasgow: James Maclehose and Sons, 1905), vol. 11, 485.

Matteo Ricci, in Louis Gallagher, SJ, trans., *China in the Sixteenth Century: The Journals of Matthew Ricci: 1583–1610* (New York: Random House, 1953), 10.

7. Athanasius Kircher, *China monumentis qua sacris qua profanes, Illustrata,* trans. Charles D. Van Tuyl (Bloomington: Indiana University Press, 1987), 207.

8. Helen Robbins, *Our First Ambassador to China: An Account of the Life of George, Earl of Macartney, with Extracts from his Letters, and the Narrative of his Experiences in China, as Told by Himself (1737–1806)* (New York: E. P. Dutton, 1908), 324.

9. George Staunton, *An Authentic Account of an Embassy from the King of Great Britain to the Emperor of China,* vol. 2, part 1 (London: G. Nicol, 1797), 184.

10. Ibid., 330.

11. Yule, *Book of Ser Marco Polo,* 285.

12. Ibid., 292.

13. Ibid., 51.

14. Jorge Luis Borges, "Franz Kafka: La metamorfosis," in Borges, *Obras Completas,* vol. 4 (Buenos Aires: Emecé, 1996), 97–99.

15. Jorge Luis Borges, "The Wall and the Books," in Borges, *Other Inquisitions, 1937–1952* (Austin: University of Texas Press, 1975), 5; translation modified.

16. Borges, "The Garden of Forking Paths," 122.

17. *Busan* [released in English under the title *Goodbye, Dragon Inn*], directed by Tsai Ming-liang (Homegreen Films, 2003).

5. Another Brick in the Wall

Epigraph: Lu Xun, "Chang cheng" [Long wall], *Lu Xun quanji* [Lu Xun's collected writings], vol. 3 (Beijing: Renmin wenxue chubanshe, 1973), 63.

1. Guo Moruo, "Fenghuang niepan" [Phoenix nirvana], in *Nüshen* [The goddess] (Beijing: Renmin wenxue chubanshe, 1957), 30–42.

2. Lin, Yü-sheng, *The Crisis of Chinese Consciousness: Radical Anti-Traditionalism in the May Fourth Era* (Madison: University of Wisconsin Press, 1979).

3. Sun Yat-sen, "Jianguo fanglüe zhi yi" [Plan for national reconstruc-

tion], in *Zhongshan quanshu* [Sun Yat-sen's collected works] (Shanghai: Zhongshan shudian, 1928), vol. 2.

4. Lu Xun, "Chang cheng."

5. David Apter and Tony Saich, *Revolutionary Discourse in Mao's Republic* (Cambridge, Mass.: Harvard University Press, 1994).

6. *Fengyun ernü* [Sons and daughters in troubled times], directed by Xu Xingzhi (1935).

7. For another translation, see Mao Zedong, *The Poems of Mao Zedong*, trans. Willis Barnstone (Berkeley: University of California Press, 2010), 69.

8. Ed Jocelyn and Andrew McEwen, *The Long March: The True Story behind the Legendary Journey that Made Mao's China* (London: Constable and Robinson, 2006).

9. *Malu tianshi* [Street angel], directed by Yuan Muzhi (Star Film Company, 1937).

10. *Maoxian wang* [King of adventure, also known as *Dr. Wai in "The Scripture with No Words"*], directed by Ching Siu-tung (1996).

11. Wu Cheng'en, *Xijou ji*; see *Journey to the West*, trans. Anthony Yu, 4 vols. (Chicago: University of Chicago Press, 1994).

12. Ibid., 4:393.

13. Richard Nixon, *Richard Nixon: Containing the Public Messages, Speeches, and Statements of the President, 1969–August 9, 1974* (Washington, D.C.: U.S. Government Printing Office, 1971–1975), 1:370.

6. A Very Queer Thing

Epigraph: *New York Times*, "Topics of the Times," June 28, 1899.

1. Hualing Nieh, *Sangqing yu taohong* (Beijing: New World Press, 1981); published in English as *Mulberry and Peach*, trans. Jane Parish Yang with Linda Lappin (New York: The Feminist Press at The City University of New York, 1998).

2. Wei Jingsheng, "Di wuge xiandaihua" [The fifth modernization], at http://weijingsheng.org/doc/en/THE%20FIFTH%20MODERNIZA TION.html.

3. Huang Xiang, "Chang cheng de zibei" [Confessions of the Great

Wall], in Huang Xiang, *A Bilingual Edition of Poetry out of Communist China by Huan Xiang,* trans. Andrew Emerson (Lewiston, N.Y.: Mellen Edwin Press, 2004), 43–44; translation quoted is mine.

4. Guannian ershiyi xingwei yishu xiaozu [Concept 21 performance art group], *Guannian ershiyi: Chang cheng* [Concept 21: The Great Wall], 1986.

5. Xu Bing, *Tianshu* [Book from the sky] (1987–1991); *Gui da qiang* [Ghosts pounding on the Wall] (1990).

6. Ma Liuming, *Fen/Ma Liuming zouxing chang cheng* [Fen/Ma Liuming walking along the Wall] (1998).

7. Lin Yilin, *Tupian laiyuan* [The result of 1,000 pieces] (1994).

8. Wang Jin, *Koumen* [Knocking at the door] (1993).

9. H. A. Schult, *Trash People at the Great Wall* (2001).

10. He Chengyao, *Kaifang chang cheng* [Opening up the Wall] (2001).

11. Wang Jin, *Bing 96 Zhongyuan* [Ice wall: '96 central China] (1996).

Epilogue

Epigraph: Yu Hua, *Brothers,* trans. Eileen Cheng-yin Chow and Carlos Rojas (New York: Pantheon, 2009), 472. Originally published as *Xiongdi* (Taipei: Rye Field, 2006); quoted passage in vol. 2, 311.

1. Meng Qingyun, lyrics, *"Chang cheng chang"* [The Long Wall is long] (2007).

Acknowledgments

My interest in the Wall originally developed as a tangent to other projects, and I am grateful to Rosalind Morris for inviting me to contribute an essay on the topic for the journal *Connect: art, politics, theory, practice*. In writing this book, I benefited immensely from the research assistance of Kock-hoo Wong, who provided support at several key stages in the project; the cartographic expertise of Philip Schwartzberg, who created the commissioned maps for the volume; and the skillful and good-humored copyediting of Julie Hagen. I am grateful to the contemporary artists who allowed me to use their work, and to the various libraries and other institutions that graciously allowed me to reproduce the maps and other images under their control. I am indebted to Wilt Idema and Wai-yee Li for reading the entire manuscript and offering many helpful comments and much good advice (some of which I was perhaps not able to fully address). I am particularly beholden to my editor, Sharmila Sen, for supporting this project from the very beginning, and for expertly shepherding it through to completion.

Finally, Eileen Cheng-yin Chow has been my rock. She not only read successive drafts of the manuscript, and was an invaluable resource for the theoretical, historical, and pop-cultural aspects of the project, but also contributed to the book in countless other, less tangible ways. To her, this volume is dedicated.

201

Index